Jean Fischer

# Morning & Evening PRAYERS for a Girl's Heart

Daily Talks with God

BARBOUR kidz
A Division of Barbour Publishing

YOU are the reason we do what we do here at Barbour Publishing. We promise that we will always use our God-given talents to produce content with you in mind—and that we will remain biblically faithful, no matter what.

*Thank you for being the heart of our business.*

---



Print ISBN 979-8-89151-285-6



Devotional thoughts and prayers are from *365 Encouraging Prayers for Girls: Morning and Evening*, published by Barbour Publishing, Inc.



Published by Barbour Publishing, Inc., 1810 Barbour Drive, Uhrichsville, Ohio 44683, www.barbourbooks.com

*Our mission is to inspire the world with the life-changing message of the Bible.*

ecpa Member of the Evangelical Christian Publishers Association

Printed in China.

002834 0226 HA

# Morning and Evening. . . Talking with God

*Evening, and morning. . .will I pray, and cry aloud: and he shall hear my voice.*

Psalm 55:17 KJV

Prayer is simply talking with God. There's no right way to do it. It's not at all complicated. You talk, God listens. That's it. Talking with God leads you into a closer relationship with Him.

The scripture verses and prayers in this book will guide you. There's a morning and evening prayer for each day of the year. But don't limit talking with God to just morning and evening. Talk with Him all day long!

MORNING

## God Is the Great I AM

*Who is like the LORD our God, who dwells on high?*

PSALM 113:5 NKJV

Dear God, You call Yourself the great I AM because You are God of heaven, earth, and everything in between. With Your great power, You created the earth and every living thing. You are perfect in every way—perfectly loving, truthful, and faithful. I know I can count on Your goodness because You never change. I am grateful for all You are, and I believe and trust in You. Amen.

EVENING

## God Gives Me Grace

*But he gives us more grace.*

JAMES 4:6 NIV

Father, thank You for Your grace—Your goodness to me even though I don't deserve it. When I do something I know is wrong, You forgive me. Whenever I'm having a hard time, when I'm angry and impatient and my behavior disappoints You, still You give me grace. You call me Your child and continue to bless me simply because You love me. Thank You, God! I praise You for Your gift of grace.

DAY 2

## MORNING

# God Says, "Come Close to Me"

*In him and through faith in him we may approach God with freedom and confidence.*

EPHESIANS 3:12 NIV

Dear Lord, I am just a small speck in the universe, yet You want me to come closer to You and Your Son, Jesus. You welcome me to come again and again to talk with You, just like I'm doing now. The closer I get to You, the surer I am about Your love for me. Remind me all day today that You are always nearby, leading and watching over me. Amen.

## EVENING

# I Want an A+ Attitude

*"For the LORD searches all hearts and understands all the intent of the thoughts."*

1 CHRONICLES 28:9 NKJV

God, You know the truth about how I think and feel. I don't want to grumble, complain, and argue, but some days that's what I do. I need Your help to adjust my attitude. Help me let go of things that upset and hurt me. Let my thoughts be about You and Your goodness. Give me an A+ attitude, Lord. Fill me with Your joy and strengthen me with Your love.

MORNING

## God Listens to Me

*"If my people, who are called by my name, will humble themselves and pray and seek my face and turn from their wicked ways, then I will hear from heaven."*

2 CHRONICLES 7:14 NIV

Dear Father, I'm grateful I can come to You this morning and talk with You. Billions of others might be praying right now, and yet You know my voice. You are always ready to listen to me and pay attention to my words. When I tell You I'm sorry for my sins—the things that displease You—You hear me and are always ready to forgive. Thank You, God, for hearing my prayer. Amen.

EVENING

## He Guards My Mind

*You will keep in perfect peace those whose minds are steadfast, because they trust in you.*

ISAIAH 26:3 NIV

God, I want to be careful about the things I see and hear because they can affect my thinking. Reading the Bible gives me a better understanding of You. I need to remember Your words. They help me fight against unhappy and unhealthy thoughts, show me right from wrong, and teach me to make good choices. I feel peaceful when I put Your words into action, because I know I'm pleasing You.

DAY 4

MORNING

# Everything Is Possible

*"Father, You can do all things."*

MARK 14:36 NLV

You—*my Father*—created the universe! When I think about that, I'm amazed. You formed the beauty of the earth, and You made our bodies with parts that work perfectly to give us life. There's nothing in heaven or on earth You can't handle. So forgive me when I worry about things. Because You made the world and everything in it, I know You have my life under control.

EVENING

# God Is My Teacher

*My son, pay attention to what I say; turn your ear to my words. Do not let them out of your sight, keep them within your heart; for they are life to those who find them and health to one's whole body.*

PROVERBS 4:20–22 NIV

Dear heavenly Father, I want You to be my teacher. You know absolutely everything, so I invite You to lead and guide me. Help me to set aside what I think is best and listen to Your directions. I'll go where You want me to go and do what You want me to do. Amen.

MORNING

# I Trust Jesus

*He gave the right and the power to become children of God to those who received Him. He gave this to those who put their trust in His name.*

John 1:12 NLV

Jesus, I trust You. Help me every day to trust You even more. I welcome You into my heart to make a home there, now and forever. You remind me that I am a child of God. Help me to keep my eyes focused on You, even when troubles come. Keep my ears tuned to Your voice, especially when I'm tempted to listen to those trying to lead me the wrong way. Amen.

EVENING

# I Show Others Mercy

*We do not use those things to fight with that the world uses. We use the things God gives to fight with and they have power. Those things God gives to fight with destroy the strong-places of the devil. We break down every thought and proud thing that puts itself up against the wisdom of God. We take hold of every thought and make it obey Christ.*

2 Corinthians 10:4–5 NLV

Jesus, when others treat me unfairly, judge me, or take something I feel I deserved, I want to get even. I want to fight for what's mine, but then I feel You urging me to show mercy—to treat others kindly, with forgiveness. It's hard for me to do that, but with Your help, I can.

MORNING

# Jesus' Gift of Forgiveness

*Because of the blood of Christ, we are bought and made free from the punishment of sin. And because of His blood, our sins are forgiven. His loving-favor to us is so rich.*

EPHESIANS 1:7 NLV

Dear Jesus, I come to You this morning thanking You for forgiveness. Whatever I do that displeases You today, I know You've already forgiven me. You died on the cross to take away my sins, all of them, past, present, and future. I don't deserve Your forgiveness, but You give it to me anyway—all the time and with all Your love. Thank You, Jesus, for this wonderful gift.

EVENING

# God Is My Strength

*Praise the LORD! For he has heard my cry for mercy. The LORD is my strength and shield. I trust him with all my heart. He helps me, and my heart is filled with joy. I burst out in songs of thanksgiving.*

PSALM 28:6–7 NLT

Lord, You give me strength, and You are my protector. You give me courage to do what I think I can't. You build me up and lead me to do things I'd never dreamed were possible. You are the friend who never leaves me. With You guiding me through life, I can do anything! I praise You, God. I'm so thankful for You, and I trust You with all my heart. Amen.

MORNING

## No Worries

*"I am leaving you with a gift—peace of mind and heart. And the peace I give is a gift the world cannot give. So don't be troubled or afraid."*

JOHN 14:27 NLT

Jesus, it's not easy finding peace in a messed-up world. But when I come to You in the stillness of this early morning, my thoughts are at rest. When I talk with You and trust in You, I set aside my worries, troubles, and fears because You have my life in Your perfect control. Lord Jesus, You are my peace. Amen.

EVENING

## God Is My Father

*And [I] will be a Father unto you, and ye shall be my sons and daughters, saith the Lord Almighty.*

2 CORINTHIANS 6:18 KJV

Dear God, You call me Your daughter. How awesome is that! Because You are my Father, I can trust You to handle every part of my life. Sometimes, I forget that. I forget how powerful You are and that You can do anything. When I forget, Father, please lead me back to putting all my faith and trust in You. You are God, and I am not—and I'm thankful that's the way it is.

DAY 8

MORNING

## Arise and Go

*The word which came to Jeremiah from the LORD, saying: "Arise and go down to the potter's house, and there I will cause you to hear My words."*

JEREMIAH 18:1–2 NKJV

Dear God, mornings are always busy with getting ready for school. Sometimes I forget how important it is to start my day talking with You. Remind me to make time to go someplace quiet and pray. Even if it means getting up earlier, I want to begin every day listening to Your voice and trusting You to guide me through the day. Amen.

EVENING

## God's Word Is True

*To the Jews who had believed him, Jesus said, "If you hold to my teaching, you are really my disciples. Then you will know the truth, and the truth will set you free."*

JOHN 8:31–32 NIV

Thank You, Lord, that everything in the Bible is true. The Bible is like a book of instructions telling how You want us to live. I want to know what's in there and live in ways that please You. Your words will never lead me down the wrong path. You will never lie to me, and I know I can count on You to always keep Your promises. Teach me, Lord. I'm ready to learn.

MORNING

## God's Mercy Is Forever

*I will be his father, and he shall be my son: and I will not take my mercy away from him.*

1 CHRONICLES 17:13 KJV

Heavenly Father, I'm thankful for Your gift of mercy. I do things that are wrong and deserving of punishment, but instead You show me love. No matter how many times I let You down, You never take Your mercy away from me. Please help me to respond with mercy when others do wrong to me. Show me how to treat them with forgiveness and love. Amen.

EVENING

## God's Word Lights the Way

*Your word is a lamp for my feet, a light on my path.*

PSALM 119:105 NIV

Lord, Your Word—the Bible—is like a lamp in the darkness. I sometimes think of it as a flashlight lighting my path through life. I don't know what's ahead, but You lead me. I'm glad that You know the right direction and that Your Word helps me stay on the right path. The Bible says You are always with me, so I don't need to be afraid. Lead the way, Lord. I will follow You.

DAY 10

MORNING

## God Comforts Me

*Blessed be God. . .the Father of mercies,*
*and the God of all comfort.*
2 Corinthians 1:3 kjv

When I am sad, Father, You comfort me. When I have bad days and everything seems to go wrong. . .when someone treats me badly. . .when things going on in the world make me worried and afraid. . .You are always with me, loving and protecting me. Thank You for caring for me. Help me lead others to You so they can experience Your comfort too.

EVENING

## God's Word Is Powerful and Alive

*God's Word is living and powerful. It is sharper than a sword*
*that cuts both ways. It cuts straight into where the soul and spirit*
*meet and it divides them. It cuts into the joints and bones.*
*It tells what the heart is thinking about and what it wants to do.*
Hebrews 4:12 nlv

Dear God, when I read the Bible, its words come alive. They have special meaning for me about what's going on in my life. Sometimes when I read, I can almost hear You saying to me, "Pay attention. There's a special message here for you." The Bible has power to help me make lasting changes in my life. When my thinking is wrong, the Bible sets it right. Thank You, God, for Your Word. Amen.

MORNING

# God Hears Me

*"Before they call I will answer;*
*while they are still speaking I will hear."*
Isaiah 65:24 niv

Lord, You always hear me. You know my heart and everything about me, even those things I can't know about my future. Before I pray, You already know what I will ask for and are answering my prayer. You know everything about everyone all the time. If the world's people were all praying at once, You would hear my prayer as if it were the only one. God, I praise You!

EVENING

# God's Word Is Useful

*All Scripture is God-breathed and is useful for teaching, rebuking, correcting and training in righteousness, so that the servant of God may be thoroughly equipped for every good work.*
2 Timothy 3:16–17 niv

Heavenly Father, please remind me to use what I learn from the Bible. Your Word can help me show others how You want them to live. I can teach them what I've learned from reading my Bible. And when I live by what the Bible teaches, I can set an example for others of how You want them to live. Help me, God, to put the Bible to good use. Amen.

# DAY 12

MORNING

## God Wants Me to Ask

*Now this is the confidence that we have in Him, that if we ask anything according to His will, He hears us.*

1 John 5:14 NKJV

God, do I ask for the right things? You say You want me to come and ask, but I don't want my prayers to be a long list of wishes as if You were some sort of genie who grants them. You answer what we ask for according to Your will, because You know what's best for us. Please reveal Your will for me. Guide me in how and for what I should pray.

EVENING

## Put Me to Work, God

*Do your best to present yourself to God as one approved, a worker who does not need to be ashamed and who correctly handles the word of truth.*

2 Timothy 2:15 NIV

Dear Lord, teach me to think about the words I read in the Bible and to put them to use in my life. Help me understand what I read and then share with my friends what I learn. Put me to work for You. I want others to know You and the truth of Your Word. Help me tell them about You in the right way so they will want to welcome You into their hearts.

MORNING

## God Loves Me!

*See what great love the Father has for us*
*that He would call us His children.*
1 John 3:1 NLV

God, You are more than a *good* Father—You are the *perfect* Father. You protect me and love me unconditionally. You always understand and forgive me, and You provide what I need. You share in everything I do and are with me always. I know I can count on You to keep Your promises and never let me down. All these things prove how much You love me. Thank You, Father. I love You too.

EVENING

## I Want to Know God's Will

*For this reason, since the day we heard about you,*
*we have not stopped praying for you. We continually*
*ask God to fill you with the knowledge of his will through*
*all the wisdom and understanding that the Spirit gives.*
Colossians 1:9 NIV

Dear Lord, I want to know Your will for me—show me what You want me to do. Give me wisdom to know what pleases You. Show me when it's right to speak and when it's best to stay quiet. Guide me to take the right path through life. Be that voice in my heart that tells me right from wrong and which way to go. Lead me, Lord, and I will follow. Amen.

DAY 14

MORNING

## More Like Jesus

*In that way, you can prove yourselves to be without blame. You are God's children and no one can talk against you, even in a sin-loving and sin-sick world. You are to shine as lights among the sinful people of this world.*

PHILIPPIANS 2:15 NLV

Dear Jesus, when I try to be more like You, my behavior gets better. When others see me doing what pleases You, I set a good example. Even when people are against me, the way I treat them shows them how You want us to treat each other. When I behave in ways that make You proud, I'm lighting the way for others to follow You.

EVENING

## Refresh Me!

*The Law of the Lord is perfect, giving new strength to the soul. The Law He has made known is sure, making the child-like wise.*

PSALM 19:7 NLV

Jesus, some days are just plain crazy. I'm so busy! Homework is hard, and I have after-school activities and things to get done at home. I feel tired and stressed out. I'm grateful to be here with You tonight. Calm me with words from the Bible. Remind me that You have everything under control. Refresh me so that in everything I do tomorrow, I will be more like You. Amen.

MORNING

## God Is Loving and Generous

*"If you then, being evil, know how to give good gifts to your children, how much more will your Father who is in heaven give good things to those who ask Him!"*
MATTHEW 7:11 NKJV

Dear God, You are so loving and generous. You give me what I don't deserve, blessing me again and again with Your goodness, love, and forgiveness. I pray that I will always be aware of Your blessings. I have nothing to offer You in return except to do my best to behave in ways that please You. Thank You for hearing me and answering my prayers. Amen.

EVENING

## God's Word Brings Me Joy

*The Laws of the Lord are right, giving joy to the heart. The Word of the Lord is pure, giving light to the eyes.*
PSALM 19:8 NLV

Lord, Your words in the Bible are right and true; they bring joy to my heart. Sometimes I need more joy. I really need it on days when things go wrong or when I just feel crabby. Reading the Bible helps me feel better. It reminds me of Your promises and how much You love me. When I'm feeling irritated and upset, I can be lifted up when I praise You. Thank You, God, for bringing me joy.

DAY 16

MORNING

# I'm Going to Live Forever!

*"They cannot die anymore. They are as the angels and are sons of God. They are children who have been raised from the dead."*

LUKE 20:36 NLV

Dear Jesus, when You died for my sins and came alive again on Easter morning, that was Your promise that I will live with You forever in heaven. Wow, I'm going to live forever! When I die, my soul—all the things that make me *me*—will live in heaven inside a new and perfect body. Because I know that, I'm not afraid of dying. Still, Jesus, I'd like to stay here for a while.

EVENING

# I Respect God's Word

*"Keep this Book of the Law always on your lips; meditate on it day and night, so that you may be careful to do everything written in it. Then you will be prosperous and successful."*

JOSHUA 1:8 NIV

Father, I respect the Bible because it is You speaking directly to me. If I have a problem, Your words in the Bible can help me solve it. Your words can comfort me and give me strength. The Bible teaches me how You want me to live. It makes me a better person. I want the Bible to be the first book I read every morning and the last book I read at night.

MORNING

## Prayer for a Rainy Day

*My voice shalt thou hear in the morning, O Lord; in the morning will I direct my prayer unto thee, and will look up.*

Psalm 5:3 KJV

Dear Lord, it's so dark and dreary this morning. I wonder what it's like there in heaven. Your love must light up everything. Are the people there walking on streets of gold that sparkle in the bright, warm heavenly light? I'll find out one day when I get there; but this morning, God, please shine Your love and light on my heart. Brighten my day. Amen.

EVENING

## God Gives Me Peace

*Grace unto you, and peace, from God our Father.*

2 Thessalonians 1:2 KJV

Thank You, Father, for the gift of Your peace. It is the only kind of peace that is true and lasts forever. When I rest in Your love, I know everything will be okay. When I have trouble, please give me an extra dose of Your peace. And when I see others who could use a little calming, help me to be ready with a word or action that leads them nearer to You.

DAY 18

MORNING

## I'm Waiting, God

*My soul wants and even becomes weak*
*from wanting to be in the house of the Lord.*
*My heart and my flesh sing for joy to the living God.*
PSALM 84:2 NLV

Dear God, there's something new I really want to do (You know what it is), but I need to get prepared before I can start. I'm ready to go. All I need is Your signal for me to begin. I'm not quite ready yet. I'm waiting for Your perfect timing. Help me to be patient. I know that someday I'll accomplish this new thing, and oh, God, how I will praise You when I've done it!

EVENING

## I Live to Please God

*You should live to please God. He is the One Who chose you to come into His holy nation and to share His shining-greatness.*
1 THESSALONIANS 2:12 NLV

Living to please You, God, is more important than anything else I accomplish in life. Help me to remember every day, all day, that my goal is to make You proud of how I behave and how I treat others. Help me, Father, to show to the world outside how You are working within me to do good things. I want it to be clear to others that You are the Lord of my life.

MORNING

## Thank You for Today

*This is the day which the LORD hath made;*
*we will rejoice and be glad in it.*
PSALM 118:24 KJV

I thank You for this day, God. Twenty-four hours are ahead of me. I have a lot to accomplish before I sleep tonight. Help me to honor You with everything I do today. Remind me to listen to Your voice in my heart that tells me to seek You for answers to my problems and to choose right decisions over wrong. Guide me today, Father. I want to please You. Amen.

EVENING

## I Want to Share You, Lord

*Let the message about Christ, in all its richness,*
*fill your lives. Teach and counsel each other with all*
*the wisdom he gives. Sing psalms and hymns and*
*spiritual songs to God with thankful hearts.*
COLOSSIANS 3:16 NLT

Lord God, I want to share You with others. I want my family and friends to know You the way I do. Show me how to share with them what's in the Bible and especially about Jesus, Your forgiveness, and heaven. If they're not interested, help me to respond with love, gentleness, and respect. I pray, Lord, that You will lead them to want to know You. I will pray for them every day. Amen.

DAY 20

MORNING

## Jesus, I Want to Please You

*How much more the blood of Christ will do! He gave Himself as a perfect gift to God through the Spirit that lives forever. Now your heart can be free from the guilty feeling of doing work that is worth nothing. Now you can work for the living God.*

Hebrews 9:14 NLV

Dear Jesus, You gave me the gift of forever life in heaven; now I want everything I do to please You. Show me the things in my life that make You proud of me, and give me courage and strength to grow those things. Help me to get rid of what disappoints You. Also help me to stay focused on You. As long as I work at pleasing You, I know I won't fail.

EVENING

## I'm Sorry, God

*Cast your cares on the Lord and he will sustain you; he will never let the righteous be shaken.*

Psalm 55:22 NIV

I'm sorry, God. Today I said things I regret. I hurt people I care about, and worse, I hurt You. Please forgive me for my angry, selfish words. I'm so glad that in the Bible You say to forgive others seventy-seven times, because I know You will forgive me even more times than that. When I misbehave, when I fall into sin, I know You will always pick me up, forgive, and love me.

MORNING

## God's Spirit Will Lead Me

*For as many as are led by the Spirit of God, they are the sons of God.*

ROMANS 8:14 KJV

Dear heavenly Father, let Your Spirit lead me today in everything I do. Help me listen for Your voice speaking in my heart, guiding me and giving me directions. Keep me from anything that leads me away from You. Please make Your Spirit so alive and active in my heart that Your voice is easy for me to hear. Guide me today in every decision I make and in all that I do. Amen.

EVENING

## What Do You Want, Jesus?

*I ask you from my heart to live and work the way the Lord expected you to live and work.*

EPHESIANS 4:1 NLV

Lord Jesus, teach me through God's Word what You expect from me. Give me courage and power to do what is right and good. Keep reminding me every day what You want from me, and then guide me down that path. You expect me to live trusting You in every way. I will trust You, Jesus. Lead me. Show me the way. I want to live up to Your expectations for me. Amen.

DAY 22

MORNING

## Father, I Praise You!

*"For then you will take pleasure in the Almighty and lift up your face to God."*
JOB 22:26 NASB

Dear Father, this morning I just want to praise You! You are awesome. You are so good to me all the time. You made mountains that almost touch the clouds, and birds as bright as rainbows, and flowers as small and perfect as a baby's fingernail—and You made me! Among all the wonderful things You made, You love me best with Your perfect, unending love. I praise You!

EVENING

## God, I Want What You Want

*Where there is no understanding of the Word of the Lord, the people do whatever they want to, but happy is he who keeps the law.*
PROVERBS 29:18 NLV

God, I want what You want. The Bible helps me understand what that is. You give me everything I need every day to accomplish what You want me to do. Help me to listen to You and follow wherever You lead. I know I can trust You, not only when I see clearly what's ahead but also when I don't know the way. Open my eyes to see what You're doing through me.

MORNING

# I'm Thankful for Small Things

*For who hath despised the day of small things? for they shall rejoice.*

ZECHARIAH 4:10 KJV

Dear Lord, today help me to be aware of the small things, the little things You do that I otherwise might miss. I promise to look more closely at nature—the earth and the sky. What hidden treasures might I find there? I will notice the little things about people that make them special and good. Thank You, Lord, for the small things. Don't let them slip by without my seeing them. Amen.

EVENING

# God Has a Purpose for Me

*Who saved us and called us with a holy calling, not according to our works, but according to His own purpose and grace, which was granted to us in Christ Jesus from all eternity.*

2 TIMOTHY 1:9 NASB

God, Your purpose for me isn't about what I want or even how hard I try to give my best to everything I do. My purpose is something You planned for me even before I was born. If I stay close to You and follow where You lead, I will begin to see my purpose unfold. What do You have planned for me, Lord? How will You use me to do Your work?

## DAY 24

MORNING

# God's Power Is Amazing!

*Then the fire of the Lord fell. It burned up the burnt gift, the wood, the stones and the dust. And it picked up the water that was in the ditch.*

1 Kings 18:38 NLV

Dear heavenly Father, Your power is amazing! You control the wind and the rain. You turn night into day. You set the moon and stars in the sky and make the sun rise and set. All of nature follows Your commands. You are everywhere all the time. There isn't anything You don't know. Lord, rain Your power down from heaven today. Bring goodness into my life. Amen.

EVENING

# I Will Set a Good Example

*Be an example to the believers with your words, your actions, your love, your faith, and your pure life.*

1 Timothy 4:12 NCV

Jesus, please help me to be a good example. I want my words and actions to be like Yours—loving, caring, faithful, and kind. Guide me to treat everyone as You would. Teach me to bring peace wherever I go. Let my behavior encourage others to behave in ways that please You. Lord, I will tell others about You because I want them to know You. I want them to welcome You into their hearts.

MORNING

## The Bible Is Forever

*O Lord, You are my God. I will praise You. I will give thanks to Your name. For You have been faithful to do great things, plans that You made long ago.*

ISAIAH 25:1 NLV

Dear God, the Bible is thousands of years old and tells stories even older. Its words and stories are forever and just as true now as they were in the days when they were written. Your words in the Bible are helpful in every situation. They teach me, comfort me, guide me, strengthen me—and sometimes they even surprise me. I praise You, God, for giving me the Bible. Thank You for its books written so long ago. Amen.

EVENING

## I Will Live What I Believe

*Walk by the Spirit, and you will not carry out the desire of the flesh.*

GALATIANS 5:16 NASB

Lord, forgive me when my choices don't line up with what I believe. I know the Bible is my guide. I want to do what it teaches, but sometimes I forget its words. Help me to keep Your Word in my heart. When I feel like doing something I know will displease You, let Your Holy Spirit speak to me. Tell me to stop! I will do my best, Lord, to live what I believe.

DAY 26

MORNING

# I Will Be a Peacemaker

*Blessed are the peacemakers: for they shall be called the children of God.*

MATTHEW 5:9 KJV

Father God, remind me that if I want the world to see me as Your child, then I need always to work for peace in the world wherever I go. Help me to be a peacemaker among my family, friends, and neighbors. Take away any angry, mean, hurtful words I might want to speak. Teach me to be a peacemaker so that others will see You through me. Amen.

EVENING

# I Am Created for Good Works

*We are God's masterpiece. He has created us anew in Christ Jesus, so we can do the good things he planned for us long ago.*

EPHESIANS 2:10 NLT

God, You have shaped me into the special person I am today. You are still working on me. I will be Your work in progress all the days of my life. You are preparing me to do Your good works. Guide me to those things You have planned for me. Give me courage in times when I think I can't or when I feel I'm not good enough. I trust You, Lord. Let's go!

MORNING

## Jesus Watches Over Me

*The Lord will keep you from all harm—he will watch over your life; the Lord will watch over your coming and going both now and forevermore.*

Psalm 121:7–8 NIV

Dear Jesus, I'm scared sometimes. I'm scared of not doing well in school. New experiences can be scary too. I'm afraid of not being good enough. I worry about my family; I want everybody to stay safe and well. I think it's normal to be scared sometimes. I'm thankful that when I'm afraid, I can be sure You are watching over me. You are my safe place, Lord.

EVENING

## God, I Will Work for You

*Do not work hard only when your owner sees you. You would be doing this just to please men. Work as you would work for Christ. Do what God wants you to do with all your heart.*

Ephesians 6:6 NLV

I want to work for You, Lord. I want to serve You with all my heart. Whatever I do, it will be for You. And when I do well, I will give You all the credit. Help me always to put You first. Open my eyes to the many different ways I can serve You. Wherever I go, whomever I meet, use me to bring Your goodness into the world. Amen.

DAY 28

MORNING

# Please Help Me to Love

*"But love those who hate you. Do good to them. Let them use your things and do not expect something back. Your reward will be much. You will be the children of the Most High. He is kind to those who are not thankful and to those who are full of sin."*

LUKE 6:35 NLV

Heavenly Father, I have a difficult time loving some of the people in my life. Your Word says that if someone treats me badly, I should react with goodness. When people are unkind, I should react with kindness. We are Your children, and You want us to love one another—especially those who are hard to love. Help me, God, to love with Your kind of love. It's not always easy. Amen.

EVENING

# Near to God's Heart

*"These people show honor to me with words, but their hearts are far from me."*

MATTHEW 15:8 NCV

Dear Lord, help me to be a true reflection of Your heart in all that I do. When I have to make a decision, help me always to ask myself, *Would this please God?* Remind me that when I do something, it shouldn't be to get attention or because I want others to praise me. Everything I do should bring honor to You. It should bring me nearer to Your heart.

MORNING

## Sometimes I Think about Dying

*But your dead will live, LORD; their bodies will rise—*
*let those who dwell in the dust wake up and shout for joy.*
ISAIAH 26:19 NIV

Lord, sometimes I think about dying. It's sad when someone passes away. It must be wonderful to be with You in heaven. But for those left here on earth, it's sad because we miss the people who aren't with us anymore. It's comforting to know that one day we can be together again with You. Until then, Lord, please comfort those who are sad. And will You say hello to anyone I know in heaven? Amen.

EVENING

## Let's All Get Along

*Put out of your life all these things: bad feelings about other people, anger, temper, loud talk, bad talk which hurts other people, and bad feelings which hurt other people.*
EPHESIANS 4:31 NLV

Father God, I need Your help getting the bad feelings out of my heart. Sometimes there are people I don't like. Help me to love them. When I get angry and my temper takes control, please help me to be calm. My words sometimes hurt others. I'm not always proud of the words that leave my lips. Help me to watch what I say. I will do my best, God, to get along with others.

DAY 30

MORNING

# Keep That Praise Coming

*Rejoice always, pray without ceasing.*

1 Thessalonians 5:16–17 NASB

Lord, You made me the beautiful person I am, and I praise You. You put my body together and made me unique—like no one else—and I praise You. You created wonderful things in nature for me to see. I praise You! You gave me people who love me and friends to have fun with. For every laugh, every hug, every gentle and caring word, I praise You. I joyfully, happily, praise You! Amen.

EVENING

# It's Important to Obey

*"If you keep my commands, you will remain in my love, just as I have kept my Father's commands and remain in his love."*

John 15:10 NIV

Father, Your Word says that if we obey Your commands, we will remain in Your love. I want my heart to obey You. I know I won't obey all Your commands all the time. No human can do that. And when I mess up, You will still love and forgive me. But I want to do my best to obey You, to please You. Help me with that, God. Encourage me to make the right decisions.

MORNING

## My Right List

*[Love] does not demand its own way. It is not irritable, and it keeps no record of being wronged.*

1 Corinthians 13:5 NLT

God, in my mind I have a list of things people have done to hurt me. Holding on to it doesn't help me to feel good. I'd rather replace it with a list of what people have done right. If I counted all the ways people are nice to me and how they show me they love me—why, that list would be very long. Help me, God, to get rid of my list of wrongs. Amen.

EVENING

## We're All God's Children

*For in him we live, and move, and have our being. . . . For we are also his offspring.*

Acts 17:28 KJV

You are my heavenly Father. You made me, and I am Your child. You love me and want what's best for me. You teach me right from wrong, guide me in everything I do, and celebrate my accomplishments. In a way, everyone on earth is my sister or brother because You made us all. God, I want us to live every day remembering and honoring You as our Father and living to please You.

MORNING

# God, Help Me Understand You

*"Call to me and I will answer you and tell you great and unsearchable things you do not know."*

JEREMIAH 33:3 NIV

You know everything, God. You see everything, and You are everywhere all the time. I don't know how You do that! There is so much about You that's too great for humans to understand. Sometimes I think I'm so smart; but compared with You, I know very little. As I'm growing up, please help me to learn more about You. Help me to become more like You.

EVENING

# I Wonder

*Dear friends, we are God's children now. But it has not yet been shown to us what we are going to be. We know that when He comes again, we will be like Him because we will see Him as He is.*

1 JOHN 3:2 NLV

Dear Jesus, I'm grateful that I'm Your child living here on earth. I can't imagine what it will be like to be Your child in heaven. I wonder what You have planned for my life here. Whatever it is, I trust You have it all under control. Someday when I get to heaven, I will be more like You than ever before. In the meantime, help me to be the best I can be. Amen.

MORNING

# Thank You, God, for Joy

*"You will go out in joy and be led forth in peace."*
ISAIAH 55:12 NIV

God, thank You for the joy You bring me every day. Help me live each day with a positive, happy attitude. Bring good things to me today, things to make me smile and laugh. Help me to see the bright side instead of thinking about my troubles. Lead me into today with joy. Let me hold on to it all day long. Wherever I go, let me bring joy with a little peace mixed in too.

EVENING

# Fill Me with Your Joy

*The LORD has done great things for us,*
*and we are filled with joy.*
PSALM 126:3 NIV

Lord, wherever You are, there is joy. Bring me near to You. The Bible says in Your presence, there is fullness of joy. So fill me with joy! Make me glad. I can't imagine being without You. You light up my life with goodness. You care about me. You comfort me. And when I pray, You really listen. I know I am loved. God, You are good to me, and I am very happy.

DAY 34

MORNING

## Jesus Brings Me Joy

*Let all who take refuge in you be glad; let them ever sing for joy. Spread your protection over them, that those who love your name may rejoice in you.*

PSALM 5:11 NIV

Jesus, I smile when I think about how much You love me. God sent You, His Son, to make a way for me to get to heaven. The first four books of the Bible's New Testament tell the story of Your life here on earth. Oh, how I wish I knew You then. But it's enough that I know You now. You are real. You are here with me always. Knowing You brings me joy.

EVENING

## I Want Wisdom!

*If you do not have wisdom, ask God for it. He is always ready to give it to you and will never say you are wrong for asking.*

JAMES 1:5 NLV

Dear Father, I have a big decision to make. You know what it is, and You know I've been thinking about it a lot. I want it to be the right decision. I need some of Your wisdom. You promise to give it to me, and You want me to ask for it. So, heavenly Father, please give me wisdom. What should I do? How should I decide? Amen.

MORNING

## Running Toward the Goal

*I've got my eye on the goal, where God is beckoning us onward—to Jesus. I'm off and running, and I'm not turning back.*

PHILIPPIANS 3:13–14 MSG

Dear God, I have a new goal. Do You want to know what it is? My goal is to tell all my friends about Jesus so they will know Him too. I probably won't tell them all at once. I'm counting on You to lead me to those who are ready to hear about Your Son. Then please give me the right words to say. Let's get going, Father. Help me reach my goal. Amen.

EVENING

## I Have a Thankful Heart

*Rejoice always, pray continually, give thanks in all circumstances; for this is God's will for you in Christ Jesus.*

1 THESSALONIANS 5:16–18 NIV

Jesus, the more I pray, the better I know You. I pray more often now, because I've come to know You as my best friend. I'm so thankful for Your friendship. My heart is full of gratefulness for all the ways You bless me. Even when things aren't going well, I'm thankful because I have You, and I know You will help me. Jesus, You are everything to me, and I love You.

# DAY 36

## MORNING

# God Is Love

*We have come to know and believe the love God has for us. God is love. If you live in love, you live by the help of God and God lives in you.*

1 John 4:16 NLV

Dear God, the Bible says You are love. Your love comes with patience, kindness, and protection. You love me with never-ending forgiveness. Because You love me so much, You will never leave me or let me down. Your love toward me is perfect, because You are perfect. Your love lives always and forever in my heart. Help me, God, to love others in the ways that You love me.

## EVENING

# I Don't Have to Be Perfect

*For the law was given through Moses; grace and truth came through Jesus Christ.*

John 1:17 NIV

Jesus, sometimes I try too hard to be perfect. Even after I do my best, I wonder if it was good enough. I can be really hard on myself. You are the only one who will ever be perfect. All I can do is my best. You only ask me to try. Remind me of that. Help me understand that in Your eyes, whether I succeed or fail, I am *always* good enough. Amen.

MORNING

## Salvation Is for Everyone!

*I am not ashamed of the Good News. It is the power of God. It is the way He saves men from the punishment of their sins if they put their trust in Him. It is for the Jew first and for all other people also.*

Romans 1:16 NLV

Dear Jesus, salvation—Your gift of forgiving us for all our sins—is our only way to heaven. I will never be ashamed to share that good news with others. When my friends and I are together having some quiet time, I will tell them how much You mean to me. I will share Your story with them. You know which of my friends are ready to hear it. Lead me to them, Lord. Amen.

EVENING

## I Am Not All That

*Do not think of yourself more highly than you ought, but rather think of yourself with sober judgment, in accordance with the faith God has distributed to each of you.*

Romans 12:3 NIV

Lord, there are things I'm really good at. I'm pleased with what I've accomplished, even proud. But that's different from being prideful. Prideful is when someone thinks they are all that. They brag about what they've done. I won't be that way. I will always work to please You; and when I accomplish something good, I will give thanks to You with a grateful heart.

DAY 38

MORNING

## God, You Are So Wise!

*Blessed be the name of God for ever and ever:*
*for wisdom and might are his.*

DANIEL 2:20 KJV

Heavenly Father, You are so wise! Nothing is secret to You. I can never understand how big and great Your wisdom is. But I'm grateful to have Your all-knowing strength and power protecting me. Today I am counting on Your wisdom and might. Whatever decisions I have to make or challenges I meet, give me wisdom to face them. Amen.

EVENING

## God Never Rests

*Do you not know? Have you not heard? The LORD is the everlasting God, the Creator of the ends of the earth. He will not grow tired or weary, and his understanding no one can fathom.*

ISAIAH 40:28 NIV

Dear God, I need a break. I need some quiet time and rest. Today was hard, but I gave it my all. I've come to You tonight to rest awhile. You never get tired, God. Nothing wears You out. You never need to slow down or sleep. So watch over me tonight, please. Build up my energy again while I rest, so that tomorrow I will be ready for a fresh, new day.

MORNING

## Jesus Is My Cheerleader

*I can do all things through*
*Christ who strengthens me.*
PHILIPPIANS 4:13 NKJV

Jesus, sometimes when I have a big goal to reach, I like to imagine You cheering me on: "What can she do? All things! Who's going to help her? Me! What am I going to do? Strengthen her!" Yay, Jesus! You are my cheerleader. You give me encouragement and strength when things get hard. Hearing Your voice inside my heart gives me courage to keep going and to hope for a win. Amen.

EVENING

## I Have Confidence

*For the Lord will be your trust.*
*He will keep your foot from being caught.*
PROVERBS 3:26 NLV

Lord, sometimes I don't feel like starting something new because I worry I might mess it up. I need to have more confidence—*trust*—in You. I know I can count on You. Even if I do mess up, it's okay with You. I trust You to give me courage to try again. Teach me to grow more confident in You. Whatever I need to do, I'm sure You will help me through it. Amen.

DAY 40

MORNING

# The Lord God of All

*He is the One Who makes the mountains and the wind. He makes His thoughts known to man. He turns the morning into darkness, and walks on the high places of the earth. The Lord God of All is His name.*

AMOS 4:13 NLV

Dear God, You created the mountains and the wind. You gave the night its darkness and the daytime light. You are Lord God of everything in heaven and on earth. When I think of who You are, I'm amazed that You created me to love and care for. You—the Lord God of all—hear me when I pray. Let me never forget how great You are and how very much You love me.

EVENING

# Foolish? Not Me!

*Blessed are those who find wisdom, those who gain understanding, for she is more profitable than silver and yields better returns than gold.*

PROVERBS 3:13–14 NIV

Father God, I can be silly, carefree, and sometimes even foolish. I forget to think before I act. I want to become wiser about what I say and do. Guide me to make right choices and behave in ways that honor You. Remind me to be thoughtful every day so my actions will please You. Help me to do what's right and to keep the promises I make to You and others. Amen.

MORNING

## I'm Under Construction

*Being confident of this, that he who began a good work in you will carry it on to completion until the day of Christ Jesus.*

PHILIPPIANS 1:6 NIV

God, I'm under construction. Sometimes I feel like there should be orange barrels all around me. I'm not done yet! I'm not who You want me to be. Each day You work on me a little more. One day I will be a woman, but even then I won't be totally complete. You'll keep working on me all the days of my life until that day when I will be perfectly complete with You in heaven.

EVENING

## "Love Your Neighbor"

*"Love your neighbor as yourself."*

MATTHEW 22:39 NIV

Jesus, You said, "Love your neighbor." Who is my neighbor? I think everyone on earth is my neighbor. You want me to care for others as much as I care for myself. Show me how to spread some love around. How can I be helpful not only to people in my neighborhood but also to strangers in my community and even around the world? Teach me to love others with Your kind of love. Amen.

DAY 42

MORNING

## When I'M Worried

*Instead of worrying, pray. Let petitions and praises shape your worries into prayers, letting God know your concerns.*

PHILIPPIANS 4:6 MSG

Dear Lord, thank You for teaching me to give my worries to You when I pray. You know what's bothering me even before I tell You, and that comforts me. I know when I tell You my worries, You already have them all worked out. When I give them to You, I'm sure they are in the best of hands. I can rest knowing that You've got this! I don't have to worry anymore.

EVENING

## Prayer Refreshes Me

*"Good will come to the man who trusts in the Lord, and whose hope is in the Lord."*

JEREMIAH 17:7 NLV

God, my days are filled with so many things: school things, after-school activities, things I have to do at home. By bedtime, my mind is so full of thoughts, I can't fall asleep. What helps is prayer. Talking with You rebuilds my strength. When I let go of the day's busyness and give it to You, I feel refreshed. Thank You for meeting me here every night, God. You are always ready and waiting. Amen.

MORNING

## Yes, I Can!

*Jesus said, "If? There are no 'ifs' among believers. Anything can happen."*

MARK 9:23 MSG

Jesus, I love reading about the amazing things You did here on earth. You walked on water, calmed a storm, and made a little boy's lunch feed a huge crowd. You healed the sick, gave sight to the blind, made those who couldn't walk, walk again. You even made dead people come alive! There's nothing You can't do. And with Your power working in me, I know I can accomplish great things. *Yes, I can!* Amen.

EVENING

## My True Identity

*God wants these great riches of the hidden truth to be made known to the people who are not Jews. The secret is this: Christ in you brings hope of all the great things to come.*

COLOSSIANS 1:27 NLV

God, You created each of us with a unique identity. How You see me on the inside might be very different from how I see myself. You know the ways I need to grow and change to become on the inside who You created me to be. Jesus is my example. He is everything I hope to become. As I try to be more like Him, You will help me discover my true identity.

## DAY 44

MORNING

# More of You, O Lord

*O magnify the LORD with me,*
*and let us exalt his name together.*

PSALM 34:3 KJV

Dear heavenly Father, I want more of You each day. Magnify Your words in the Bible—make them clearer to me and easier to understand. Build up my faith and trust in You. Grow the number of friends I have who know and love You so we can talk about You together and praise You together. God, You are the biggest and best part of my life. Amen.

EVENING

# I Am God's Child

*The Spirit of God, who raised*
*Jesus from the dead, lives in you.*

ROMANS 8:11 NLT

Wow, God. You call me Your child! Before You gave me parents here on earth, You were already my Father. You created me, planned my whole life, decided where I would live and who my mom and dad would be. You've been with me from the moment You decided to make me Your child, and You will love and stay with me forever. I'm glad that I'm Yours. Amen.

MORNING

## My Savior

*The One Who bought us and saves us, the Lord of All is His name, the Holy One of Israel.*

ISAIAH 47:4 NLV

Dear Jesus, You are my Savior—the one who rescues me. You saved me from every sin that separated me from God. When You died on the cross, my sin died with You. Accepting You as my Savior means I will be ready to enter heaven one day. I don't need to worry about forgiveness when I sin because, thanks to You, God has already forgiven me. Thank You, Jesus! Amen.

EVENING

## God Bless This House

*The punishment of the Lord is on the house of the sinful, but He makes good come to the house of those who are right with Him.*

PROVERBS 3:33 NLV

Father God, bless my house and everyone who lives here. Stay with us always. Protect us and fill up each room with Your love. Keep us from doing things that displease You. Make our home a peaceful place, a place where others always feel welcome. Please guide us to share You with our guests. Give us the right words to tell them about Jesus and His gift of forgiveness. Amen.

MORNING

## Babies

*He tends his flock like a shepherd: he gathers the lambs in his arms and carries them close to his heart; he gently leads those that have young.*

Isaiah 40:11 NIV

Jesus, I enjoy watching animals care for their babies. You created them to lovingly protect their little ones and keep them comfortable and warm. Animal parents provide food for their children. They'll risk their lives to be sure their young are safe. Jesus, You do all that for us and so much more. We are Your babies! You carry us close to Your heart and meet all our needs. Thank You! I love You. Amen.

EVENING

## A Time for Every Season

*To everything there is a season,*
*a time for every purpose under heaven.*

Ecclesiastes 3:1 NKJV

The Bible says there is a time for everything. Just as there are seasons in nature, our lives go through seasons. Some are happy, others sad. Sometimes we reach goals. Other times we don't quite get there. I want to celebrate every season of my life. I celebrate them because You are with me through them all. You bless me with goodness and dry my tears when I'm sad. Thank You, God, for seasons. Amen.

MORNING

# Trouble

*O God Who saves us, help us for the honor of Your name. Take us out of trouble and forgive our sins, for the honor of Your name.*

PSALM 79:9 NLV

O God, I have trouble sometimes staying away from trouble! I know certain things are wrong, and I do them anyway. I want to please You, but I make choices to please myself instead. I know You have already forgiven me. Still, I want to tell You I'm sorry. Will You help me, God? I want to stay out of trouble. I want to behave in ways that honor You.

EVENING

# Encouraging Words

*Gracious words are a honeycomb, sweet to the soul and healing to the bones.*

PROVERBS 16:24 NIV

Dear God, when people say encouraging things to me like "You can do it," "I believe in you," and "I see you working really hard!" I feel good. I love hearing those words, but sometimes I forget that I can encourage others too. Every day I want to use my words to encourage someone. Will You help me, Lord? Show me who needs some encouragement. Then give me the right words to say.

## MORNING

# I Will be Brave!

*"The LORD will cause your enemies who rise against you to be defeated before your face; they shall come out against you one way and flee before you seven ways."*

DEUTERONOMY 28:7 NKJV

God, I was reading in my Bible about David and Goliath. David was a young shepherd boy. Goliath was a big, mean enemy soldier. When all the soldiers fighting Goliath's army were afraid, David bravely stood up to the giant man. With one well-aimed stone, he knocked the giant down. That was Your power working through David. When enemies come my way, give me power like David's to knock them down. I will be brave! Amen.

## EVENING

# A Lesson in-Ants!

*The ants are not a strong people,*
*but they prepare their food in the summer.*

PROVERBS 30:25 NASB

Lord, sometimes You use nature to teach us. There are lessons in the smallest of things. Ants, for example. Ants are always busy. They store food, preparing for winter. They work well together as a team. I never see ants hanging around doing nothing. They're always working hard and getting things done. I think You want me to be a hard worker too and someone who works well with others. Thanks for the lesson, Father! Amen.

MORNING

## Clean and Fresh

*Jesus answered, "Unless I wash you,*
*you have no part with me."*
JOHN 13:8 NIV

Jesus, when You died on the cross, You took my sins away. Sin made us look dirty in God's sight. He didn't like seeing His children covered in shameful words and behavior, so He sent us You! We can have all of You just by asking. I want *all* of You! Thank You, Jesus, for making me clean again. Thank You for washing away my sin.

EVENING

## I'll Think About Jesus

*Since Christ suffered while he was in his body, strengthen yourselves with the same way of thinking Christ had. The person who has suffered in the body is finished with sin.*
1 PETER 4:1 NCV

Jesus, You really suffered when You died for my sin. People said hateful things to You. They nailed You to a cross and left You there to die. That must have hurt so much. The worst of my days are nothing compared with how You suffered for me. I won't die if everything doesn't go my way! So, on bad days, remind me of Your suffering on the cross, and help me to be grateful. Amen.

MORNING

## When I Can't Pray

*In the same way, the Holy Spirit helps us where we are weak. We do not know how to pray or what we should pray for, but the Holy Spirit prays to God for us with sounds that cannot be put into words.*

ROMANS 8:26 NLV

Dear God, I don't know how to pray this morning. A lot is going on. I feel like crying because I don't even know what to ask You for. The Bible says when I don't have the words to pray, Your Holy Spirit will pray for me. I need that today, Lord. Let Your Spirit speak for me. You know best what I need. Amen.

EVENING

## Look Ahead

*"When the Spirit of truth comes, he will guide you into all truth. He will not speak on his own but will tell you what he has heard. He will tell you about the future."*

JOHN 16:13 NLT

Father, when I look at what happened a while ago, I see that things didn't turn out as I expected. I messed up. I learned from that what not to do next time. You have a plan for me. I have a great life up ahead. So I'm not going to worry about my past mistakes. Instead, I'll look to the future with joy! I can't wait to see what You have there waiting for me.

MORNING

## Seeking God

*"For the LORD searches all hearts and understands all the intent of the thoughts. If you seek Him, He will be found by you."*

1 CHRONICLES 28:9 NKJV

God, the Bible says if I seek You, I will find You. Every day I try to keep my mind set on You. I look for You all around me: in nature, in the kind ways people treat me, in the little lessons I learn about living right. You search my heart and know my every thought. Help my thoughts to line up with what You want for me. My goal is to please You.

EVENING

## Sharing My Blessings

*"Everyone shall give as he is able, in accordance with the blessing of the LORD your God which He has given you."*

DEUTERONOMY 16:17 NASB

Lord, I'm grateful for all the ways You've blessed me. You are so good to me! Please, will You use me to bless others? I can give my time if that's what someone needs. I'm helpful with chores. Maybe someone needs my help. I have more than what I need, so I can share. I'm good at lots of things. How can I use my talents to bless others? Show me what to do.

## DAY 52

### MORNING

# I Will Honor God's Name

*Give to the Lord the honor of His name.*
*Bring a gift and come into His holy place.*
PSALM 96:8 NLV

Heavenly Father, sometimes I hear people use Your name in ways that don't honor You. Your name—God, Jesus, Holy Spirit—is holy. It should always be said with respect. Using Your name in an angry way or as a swear word is never right. Whenever Your name is spoken, it is almost like a prayer sent straight to Your ears. Lord, I will always be respectful and honor Your name. Amen.

### EVENING

# The More I Give Back

*"Bring to the storehouse a full tenth of what you earn so there will be food in my house. Test me in this," says the* LORD *All-Powerful. "I will open the windows of heaven for you and pour out all the blessings you need."*
MALACHI 3:10 NCV

Dear God, I've noticed that when I do my best to bless others, I'm blessed in return. I'm blessed with hugs and thankful words, and that makes me feel good. I love how You help me help others. It makes me feel even nearer to You, and that's a blessing too! Your power is working through me to reach others. Help me to keep the blessings going. Amen.

MORNING

# I Love My Life

*"I call heaven and earth to speak against you today. I have put in front of you life and death, the good and the curse. So choose life so you and your children after you may live."*

DEUTERONOMY 30:19 NLV

Lord God, instead of looking at all I don't have, I look at all You've blessed me with. The list of the blessings in my life is endless. Thank You so much for my life and every good thing in it. This morning I'm thinking about all the special people in my life and the things and activities that bring me joy. I am blessed. I love my life! Amen.

EVENING

# Set Free

*"It will be that whoever calls on the name of the Lord will be saved from the punishment of sin."*

JOEL 2:32 NLV

Jesus, when I misbehave and do something against the rules, I have to face the consequences. Usually, I lose a privilege or one of my things is taken away for a while. But when I sin, Lord, one thing is for sure—You won't hold that sin against me. All I have to do is call Your name, and I know You've already forgiven me. You took the punishment I deserved and set me free.

DAY 54

## MORNING

# God Is Strong

*He will come and feed His flock in the strength of the Lord, in the great power of the name of the Lord His God.*

MICAH 5:4 NLV

Dear God, some problems seem so big. I feel powerless against them. But when I feel weak, I remind myself that You are strong. All I need to do is call on You for help, and You will give me strength. Your power can help me solve my problem right away or give me enough strength to put up with it for a while. I can always count on You, God. Thank You.

## EVENING

# Jesus and Me

*All praise to God, the Father of our Lord Jesus Christ, who has blessed us with every spiritual blessing in the heavenly realms because we are united with Christ.*

EPHESIANS 1:3 NLT

Heavenly Father, Jesus is my best friend. He took the punishment for all the wrong things I'll ever do in my life. He loves me that much! His love blesses me every day. I feel Jesus with me always. He guides me through my days and helps me to do what's right. I end every day spending quiet time talking with Him. I'm grateful for Jesus. Thank You, God, for giving me Your Son. Amen.

MORNING

# My Protector

*Keep me as the apple of your eye;*
*hide me in the shadow of your wings.*
PSALM 17:8 NIV

Jesus, my class visited a farm, and when a mother hen saw us coming toward her, she pulled her chicks close to her and covered them with her wings. She protected them from being afraid. Jesus, You are like that mother hen. When I am afraid, I imagine You putting Your arms around me and holding me tight. You love me, and You are my protector. You are my safe place, Lord. Amen.

EVENING

# My Job

*Do not do wrong to repay a wrong, and do not insult to repay an insult. But repay with a blessing, because you yourselves were called to do this so that you might receive a blessing.*
1 PETER 3:9 NCV

Dear God, when someone treats me badly, I feel like treating them the same way. But that's not what You want me to do. My job is to bless others. I'm supposed to be an extension of You. Reading the Bible helps me know what You'd want me to do. It isn't always easy loving people who are mean and rude, but I'll do my best. Please help me, God. Amen.

MORNING

# Singing God's Name

*I will praise the name of God with a song,*
*and will magnify him with thanksgiving.*
PSALM 69:30 KJV

Heavenly Father, I love hearing choirs sing in concerts and at church. All the voices—low, medium, high—blend to make the most beautiful music. If choirs sound so good here on earth, I can only imagine how amazing they sound in heaven. This morning I will sing my praises to You, Lord. It doesn't matter if I sing well or not. My voice is always music to Your ears.

EVENING

# Joy!

*Our mouths were filled with laughter,*
*our tongues with songs of joy.*
PSALM 126:2 NIV

Dear Lord, thank You for the gift of laughter! Thank You for the joy You bring into my life through hanging out with my friends, special celebrations, having fun with my family, and even a good night's sleep. I think You must enjoy seeing me happy, because You're always adding fun things to my life. I wonder what kind of joy You have planned for me tomorrow. I can't wait to find out. Amen.

MORNING

## My Plan for Today

*The Lord God, the Holy One of Israel, has said, "In turning away from sin and in rest, you will be saved. Your strength will come by being quiet and by trusting."*

ISAIAH 30:15 NLV

Lord God, Your Word always holds good advice. Today's verse tells me how to begin my day. I will focus on staying away from sin—those things that displease You. If I get stressed out today, I'll take a minute or two to be alone and quiet with You. I know You will give me strength when I put all my trust in You. Amen.

EVENING

## Bedtime Praise

*May the peoples praise you, God; may all the peoples praise you. The land yields its harvest; God, our God, blesses us.*

PSALM 67:5–6 NIV

God, when I pray at bedtime, I always begin by praising You. I have much to be grateful for. All day today, You met my needs. I felt You helping me and guiding me through things I wasn't sure of. You gave me strength to accomplish what I thought I couldn't. Now I will lie down and sleep in peace because You are with me, watching over me through the night. Lord, I praise You.

## DAY 58

### MORNING

## A Daily Blessing

*"May the Lord bring good to you and keep you. May the Lord make His face shine upon you, and be kind to you. May the Lord show favor toward you, and give you peace."*

NUMBERS 6:24–26 NLV

Dear God, You gave the words in Numbers 6:24–26 to Moses as a blessing to speak to Your people. This blessing is also for me today. I trust You to be good to me and keep me well protected in Your care. You will be watching over me, lighting my way. I know I can count on Your kindness, because I am Your child. You love me and will bring me peace.

### EVENING

## God Is Right and Fair

*I, the Lord, love what is right and fair. I hate stealing and what is wrong.*

ISAIAH 61:8 NLV

Lord, I broke a house rule last night for the second time. Mom scolded me and said, "I've been very fair with you." She *was* fair, God. I should have learned from the first time. You are like my mom. You hate what's wrong. You are always fair with me. You love it when I do what's right. I'll try harder, God. I promise. Thanks for being patient and forgiving me. Amen.

MORNING

# Christ Is All I Need

*He answered me, "I am all you need. I give you My loving-favor. My power works best in weak people." I am happy to be weak and have troubles so I can have Christ's power in me.*

2 Corinthians 12:9 NLV

Dear Jesus, I have everything I need to start this day because I have You! I have a busy day ahead at school and after school. I'm worried about a few things, but I know they will turn out okay because Your power is working through me. Your power seems to work best when I have troubles or am unsure of myself. You will never let me down. I'm ready, Jesus. Let's go!

EVENING

# One Little Word

*People. . .begged him to let the sick just touch the edge of his cloak, and all who touched it were healed.*

Matthew 14:35–36 NIV

Jesus, when I'm sad or sick and need some healing, I turn to You. I don't have to go to a quiet place to pray. I don't have to beg for Your help with a long prayer, saying just the right words. Just one little word like "help" is enough. You will hear that tiny prayer and fill me up with Your love. With You in my heart, nothing can harm me. Amen.

## DAY 60

### MORNING

# Tasty Words

*Your words were found and I ate them. And Your words became a joy to me and the happiness of my heart. For I have been called by Your name, O Lord God of All.*

JEREMIAH 15:16 NLV

Father God, the Bible is for everyone; but when I read its words, they speak to me like they were written just for me. Reading Your words is another way You and I connect. Your words are a treat! They make me happy. Sometimes I can't get enough of them. I gobble them up and want even more. Thank You, God, for the Bible. Thank You for using it to speak to me. Amen.

### EVENING

# Second Chances

*Obey the LORD your God so that all these blessings will come and stay with you.*

DEUTERONOMY 28:2 NCV

Lord God, Your blessings are more than I deserve; still, You keep on blessing me. Every day I do things that I know are sinful. But when I disobey, You give me a second chance, a third, a fourth. . . When I'm Your disobedient child, You keep on blessing me with forgiveness. Help me to do better, God. I want You to see how grateful I am for Your blessings. I love You. Amen.

MORNING

## Celebrate Jesus

*Nehemiah said, "Go and enjoy choice food and sweet drinks, and send some to those who have nothing prepared. This day is holy to our Lord. Do not grieve, for the joy of the LORD is your strength."*

NEHEMIAH 8:10 NIV

Jesus, I complain about things. On days when nothing goes right, I grumble and I'm not much fun to be around. Complaining makes me feel worse. It sucks the joy out of me. This morning's scripture verse reminds me that You are my reason to celebrate each day. You say, "Enjoy some food and sweet drinks. Share with others." Today, Jesus, and every day, I celebrate because I find joy in knowing You. Amen.

EVENING

## Put God First

*"No one can have two bosses. He will hate the one and love the other. Or he will listen to the one and work against the other. You cannot have both God and riches as your boss at the same time."*

MATTHEW 6:24 NLV

God, I like nice things. I want to have the newest and best. If I get something I love, I show it off to my friends. Sometimes my things become more important to me than You are. That's wrong, Lord. I should be grateful for what I have and thankful to You for the special things I receive. You are more important than any of my things or anything else in my life. Forgive me.

MORNING

## Do It Your Way, Lord

*The effective, fervent prayer of a righteous man avails much.*

JAMES 5:16 NKJV

Lord, when I pray, asking for things, I know You will give me exactly what I need, but it might not be what I want. Sometimes You say no because You have something even better waiting for me in the future. I can't see what's ahead, but I trust You. When I end my prayer with "Amen," what I really mean is "Do it Your way." So, Lord, do it Your way. Amen.

EVENING

## When I'm Weak, I'm Strong

*I receive joy when I am weak. I receive joy when people talk against me and make it hard for me and try to hurt me and make trouble for me. I receive joy when all these things come to me because of Christ. For when I am weak, then I am strong.*

2 CORINTHIANS 12:10 NLV

It's true, Jesus. When I'm weak, I'm strong. Whenever there's something I think I can't do, or when friends say mean things to me, or when trouble comes my way, You give me strength. I'm like the little shepherd boy, David, standing up to that giant soldier, Goliath. I might be little and weak; but faith in You, Jesus, makes me strong. Thank You for standing up for me and giving me some of Your power. Amen.

MORNING

# Sharing God's Holiness

*So we will be holy as He is holy.*

HEBREWS 12:10 NLV

Father, fill my heart with some of Your holiness—Your perfect goodness and power. Make Your Spirit alive in my heart whenever I pray, read Your Word, or just sit quietly with You. Make me aware of You always, wherever I go, whatever I do. When I get too busy to spend time with You, please invite me back to where You are. I need You, God. I want You. Amen.

EVENING

# I Want to Be Like Jesus

*We know that God makes all things work together for the good of those who love Him and are chosen to be a part of His plan. God knew from the beginning who would put their trust in Him. So He chose them and made them to be like His Son.*

ROMANS 8:28–29 NLV

Lord, I know You will work out everything in my life according to Your plan for me. I'm happy that I am Your child, and I trust in Your love. When You made me Your child, You made me to be like Your Son, Jesus. Please help me to become more like Him. Give me some of His gentleness and strength so I can use it every day to serve others. Thank You, God. Amen.

## DAY 64

### MORNING

# Jesus, I Need You

*On the last and greatest day of the festival, Jesus stood and said in a loud voice, "Let anyone who is thirsty come to me and drink. Whoever believes in me, as Scripture has said, rivers of living water will flow from within them."*

John 7:37–38 NIV

Jesus, some days I don't know exactly what I need. I want something to make me feel happy or to make me ready to do something I've been putting off. I want a push in the right direction. Jesus, You are my helper. I want more of You. In my heart, it feels like when I want a cold drink of water after running and playing hard. I need You. Come to me. Amen.

### EVENING

# My Body

*I ask you to keep away from all the sinful desires of the flesh. These things fight to get hold of your soul.*

1 Peter 2:11 NLV

Dear God, You created my body. You made it exactly the way You wanted it. It's my responsibility to use it in ways that honor You. I'll do my best to keep it clean and in shape. I'll think about the clothes I wear, and I will dress to honor You. You gave me a strong body, and I will use it to serve You by helping others. Thank You, God, for my body. Amen.

MORNING

# God Is Light

*God is light, and in him is no darkness at all.*

1 JOHN 1:5 KJV

Father God, You are the brightest light. There is no darkness in You at all. There is absolutely no sin in You because You are everything perfect and good. Your love is like sunshine, bright and warm. When people look toward You and heaven, all the darkness—all the bad things on earth—melts away. Shine brightly on me, Lord. Let Your light shine through me so others will see it. Amen.

EVENING

# I'll Work Even Harder

*They were just trying to intimidate us, imagining that they could discourage us and stop the work. So I continued the work with even greater determination.*

NEHEMIAH 6:9 NLT

Dear Lord, You know the goal I'm working toward. One of my friends said to me, "You can't do that! You're not good enough." I said, "I *am* good enough! God will give me all the strength I need." Now I want to work even harder to meet my goal. I want my friend to see You working through me. Together we will do this, Lord! Nothing will discourage me. Amen.

# DAY 66

## MORNING

# The Lord Is My Rock

*The LORD is my rock, and my fortress, and my deliverer; my God, my strength, in whom I will trust; my buckler, and the horn of my salvation, and my high tower.*

PSALM 18:2 KJV

Heavenly Father, Your power and strength are perfect. You are like a huge fort made of the strongest steel. Nothing can get past You. You are like a great mountain made of stone. When trouble comes at me, it meets You first. You are in control, my protector; You shield me from danger. I shouldn't be afraid because I am safe with You, my God and my rock. Amen.

## EVENING

# I Won't Be Afraid

*Though an army may encamp against me, my heart shall not fear.*

PSALM 27:3 NKJV

Dear God, new places sometimes frighten me. Taking that first step into the unknown makes my heart beat fast. I want to turn around and run to where I feel safe. But then I remind myself that You are my safe place. You are wherever I am. You are already in that new place I'm so afraid of. Whatever is up ahead, God, it's going to be okay because You'll be with me. Let's go!

MORNING

## Jesus Is Welcome Here

*"Behold, I stand at the door and knock; if anyone hears My voice and opens the door, I will come in to him and will dine with him, and he with Me."*

REVELATION 3:20 NASB

Lord, when You lived on earth, You traveled all the time. Your home happened to be wherever You stopped for a while. People welcomed You into their homes. They loved having You as a houseguest. Dear Jesus, my house is Your home too. You are always welcome here. You fill our home with blessings and love. You bring us joy and peace. Come, Lord Jesus, be our guest. Amen.

EVENING

## God Knows Best

*Paul would not listen to us. So we stopped begging him and said, "May whatever God wants be done."*

ACTS 21:14 NLV

Father God, in the Bible, Your follower Paul always turned to You for advice. When his friends told him what they thought he should do, Paul wasn't quick to act on what they said. He talked with You. He wanted what *You* wanted. That's how I'm going to pray. It's okay to tell You what I want, but I'll end my prayers with "God, may Your will be done." Amen.

DAY 68

MORNING

## Guaranteed Blessing

*"The Lord will guarantee a blessing on everything you do."*

Deuteronomy 28:8 NLT

Lord God, the Bible says You actually guarantee a blessing on everything I do! What an awesome promise that is. I can count on all Your promises. So I have confidence this morning that You will be with me in everything I do, blessing me at every turn. I know I miss noticing many of Your blessings, so I'll keep my eyes open for them today. Thank You, God.

EVENING

## Waiting

*Lead me in thy truth, and teach me: for thou art the God of my salvation; on thee do I wait all the day.*

Psalm 25:5 KJV

Father in heaven, it's hard when I'm praying for something I want badly and You tell me to wait. I know, though, that waiting on You is good. Waiting means You have something to teach me; or maybe I'm not ready yet to receive what I've asked for; or You have something different in Your plan for me. So, Lord, I will wait. Please help me to be patient. Amen.

MORNING

## Out of Sight

*The proud religious law-keepers asked when the holy nation of God would come. Jesus said to them, "The holy nation of God is not coming in such a way that can be seen with the eyes."*

LUKE 17:20 NLV

Father, someday Jesus will come back to earth. We don't know when. Many things You hold secret. We know, though, that although we can't see it with our eyes, Your kingdom is all around us. Your kingdom is in everything good. It's in all the people working to serve You. It's in everything helpful and hopeful. Let me serve You, God. I want others to see Your kingdom through me.

EVENING

## Jesus Is My Help

*Our help is in the name of the LORD,*
*who made heaven and earth.*

PSALM 124:8 NKJV

I don't have to look any further for someone to help me, Jesus, because You are the help I need. I trust You. Your power helps me meet every challenge. It stands up to trouble that gets in my way. You know the plan for my life, and You will give me everything I need to work that plan. Help me trust You even more and always turn to You first for help. Amen.

# DAY 70

## MORNING

## Here I Am, Lord

*Therefore, I urge you, brothers and sisters, in view of God's mercy, to offer your bodies as a living sacrifice, holy and pleasing to God—this is your true and proper worship.*

ROMANS 12:1 NIV

Lord, I give everything I am to You this morning. I want to please You, because I love You with all my heart. Use me to serve You today. Whether it's through my words or actions, use me. Show me how I can use the strength You've blessed me with to help those who are weak. Here I am, Lord. I am Yours. I give all that I have to You.

## EVENING

## God's Power Makes Me Strong

*I pray that God's great power will make you strong, and that you will have joy as you wait and do not give up.*

COLOSSIANS 1:11 NLV

Father, I keep trying, but so far I'm not getting anywhere. I keep waiting, thinking that I'll get better at what I need to do. But so far I'm not strong enough to reach my goal. I won't give up, though, because I know Your power is working inside me. When You know I'm ready, I'll sail right through what I want to accomplish. What a happy, joyful day that will be!

MORNING

## I Can Be a Disciple

*He went throughout every city and village, preaching and shewing the glad tidings of the kingdom of God.*

LUKE 8:1 KJV

Dear Jesus, after You went back to heaven, Your disciples carried on Your work here on earth. Their purpose was to tell others the good news about You—that You came to take the punishment for our sins and promise us forever life in heaven. I can be a disciple too. I can make it my purpose to tell others about You. Teach me how to do that, Lord. I'm ready. Amen.

EVENING

## God Is My Protector

*I will not trust in my bow, nor shall my sword save me. But You have saved us from our enemies, and have put to shame those who hated us. In God we boast all day long, and praise Your name forever.*

PSALM 44:6–8 NKJV

Dear God, I don't need strong walls or weapons or an army to protect me, because You are my protector. Faith in You is all I need. When people treat me badly or say mean things about me, I trust You to take care of it. You will somehow someday put them to shame. I will praise You, God. All day and all night I will praise You. I will praise You forever! Amen.

DAY 72

MORNING

# God Will Never Leave Me

*Everyone deserted me. May it not be held against them. But the Lord stood at my side and gave me strength. . . . And I was delivered.*

2 TIMOTHY 4:16–17 NIV

Lord, some people will be in my life always. Others will come and go. It hurts when people leave me. But You are always with me. Today, every day of my life, and then in heaven, You will be with me forever. All I need is You. I feel You in my heart, loving me and giving me power to be strong no matter what comes my way. Thank You for never leaving me.

EVENING

# God Is My GPS

*Your ears shall hear a word behind you, saying, "This is the way, walk in it," whenever you turn to the right hand or whenever you turn to the left.*

ISAIAH 30:21 NKJV

Father, if I pay attention to Your words, I don't have to worry about my life going in the wrong direction. You are like a GPS. Your Holy Spirit speaks to my heart, "Go this way," or "Stop! Turn around." I trust You to know the way I should go. It's not always clear for me to see, but You know if the path ahead is safe and right. I trust You to guide me. Amen.

MORNING

## Be Right with God

*For the holy nation of God is not food and drink. It is being right with God. It is peace and joy given by the Holy Spirit.*

ROMANS 14:17 NLV

Heavenly Father, the world is a big and busy place. It can be messy sometimes. All the noise makes it hard to remember to put You first and listen to Your voice. Your kingdom isn't built on things of this world. It's built on us being right with You. God, when I listen to You and follow You, I find peace and joy. Your kingdom exists in my heart.

EVENING

## My Hope Is in You

*"And now, Lord, what do I wait for? My hope is in You."*

PSALM 39:7 NKJV

Dear God, I'm not good at running toward new challenges. I drag my feet, worrying that maybe the task is too great. But that's not how You want me to react. You want me to put all my faith in You and be bold. You want me to face my challenges head-on with You guiding me. So what am I waiting for? Father, I won't be afraid. My hope is in You.

DAY 74

## MORNING

# So Many Questions

*And he said, So is the kingdom of God,*
*as if a man should cast seed into the ground.*
MARK 4:26 KJV

Father God, what does today's scripture verse mean? Is Your kingdom like someone casting seed on the ground? Does this mean I can find Your kingdom everywhere, scattered throughout the world? When I read the Bible, I have so many questions. I often run to You for answers. Open my eyes to the meaning of Your words. Give me wisdom. Help me to understand more about Your kingdom. Amen.

## EVENING

# Make Me Bold

*On the day I called, You answered me;*
*You made me bold with strength in my soul.*
PSALM 138:3 NASB

Lord, I could use a little more boldness. Sometimes I'm afraid to speak up about things I believe in. I'm even a little shy telling others about You. I don't want my doubts and fears to become bigger than my faith. Give me strength to do what You want me to do. Help me to stand up for what's right and to never be afraid to speak the truth. Amen.

MORNING

## Be Still

*"Be still, and know that I am God."*
PSALM 46:10 NIV

Dear God, I don't know why I get so worked up over things I can't control. You are always exactly where You want to be—*with me*! When I'm worried or afraid, all I need to do is be still and let You be in charge. Help me, please, to slow down and put all my trust in You. There's nothing You can't do, so I will just wait, relax, and be still. Amen.

EVENING

## By Faith, I Go

*By faith Abraham, when he was called, obeyed by going out to a place which he was to receive for an inheritance; and he left, not knowing where he was going.*
HEBREWS 11:8 NASB

Father God, the Bible is filled with stories of people like Abraham who stepped out in faith not knowing where You were taking them. They trusted You, listened to You, and obeyed. Faith doesn't have a map. It means allowing You to lead all the time. So lead me, God. I will walk in faith, following You, not knowing where we're going, because I trust in You.

DAY 76

MORNING

# A Mustard Seed

*[The kingdom of God] is like a grain of mustard seed, which, when it is sown in the earth, is less than all the seeds that be in the earth.*

MARK 4:31 KJV

Father, I learned in church that a tiny mustard seed can grow into a bush twenty feet tall! Your Word compares the growth of that little seed to how faith grows. If even a tiny bit of faith is in my heart, it can grow and keep growing all the days of my life. Lord, make my heart a place that is excellent for growing my faith. I want my faith in You to be big and powerful, like Your kingdom.

EVENING

# God Looks at the Heart

*The LORD said to Samuel, "Do not consider his appearance or his height, for I have rejected him. The LORD does not look at the things people look at. People look at the outward appearance, but the LORD looks at the heart."*

1 SAMUEL 16:7 NIV

God, I want to be more like You and look at what's inside a person's heart instead of what they look like on the outside. Too often what I see first is how tall or short some people are, how they do their hair, how they dress. . . But that's not what You see. You see what's inside—things like goodness, caring, and helpfulness. Help me, Lord, to see with Your eyes. Amen.

MORNING

## A Special Supper

*All the days of the suffering are hard,*
*but a glad heart has a special supper all the time.*
PROVERBS 15:15 NLV

Dear Jesus, my mom always knows if I'm having a hard time. Sometimes she helps me feel better by preparing a special supper with my favorite foods. You are like an all-the-time special supper. When things are going wrong, You work to bring me joy. You pour Your love into me. I think You even give people around me ideas to help me feel better. Lord, You make my heart glad.

EVENING

## Take Delight in the Lord

*Take delight in the LORD, and he will*
*give you the desires of your heart.*
PSALM 37:4 NIV

Lord, I looked up that word *delight*. It means "great joy or happiness." I think today's scripture verse means that if I look to You for happiness, You will bless me. Your blessings always make me happy. I think You've put dreams inside me that someday will become real. I can't wait to see all the wonderful things You have planned for me. Lord, I take delight in You. You bring me joy.

DAY 78

MORNING

## God Gives Me Mercy and Grace

*So let us come boldly to the throne of our gracious God. There we will receive his mercy, and we will find grace to help us when we need it most.*

HEBREWS 4:16 NLT

My Father, You are quick to show mercy. You are God. You could punish me for my sins. But instead, You always love and forgive me. You show me grace, giving me all the blessings I don't deserve. I try to imagine You sitting on Your throne, ruling heaven. Big. Powerful. The one and only God. You are greater than anything I can imagine. And yet You know and love me—I am Your child.

EVENING

## God Loves Kids!

*Verily I say unto you, Whosoever shall not receive the kingdom of God as a little child, he shall not enter therein.*

MARK 10:15 KJV

Dear God, You love kids! You love that we have questions and come to You for answers. You love that we don't let anything get in the way of our trust in You. You delight in our firsts, and You celebrate our accomplishments. Best of all, You always have time for us. Our lives are fresh and new. So open Your earthly kingdom to us. We're ready to explore and discover. Amen.

MORNING

## Laughter and Singing

*Then our mouth was filled with laughter, and our tongue with singing. Then they said among the nations, "The LORD has done great things for them."*

PSALM 126:2 NKJV

Lord God, each day You provide fun things for me to do. You've given me good friends. We hang out, and sometimes we like being silly. We laugh until our sides hurt! We ride our bikes, go to the park, have sleepovers, sing, dance, play games, make cool things. . . Thank You, Lord, for my friends and for bringing so much joy and happiness into my life. Amen.

EVENING

## God's Kingdom Is Real

*For the kingdom of God is not in word, but in power.*

1 CORINTHIANS 4:20 KJV

Dear God, when my little sister and I play together, we imagine we are princesses living in a pretend kingdom. Pretending is fun. But Your kingdom is real. You created earth and everything in it. You rule over Your earthly kingdom. Nothing and no one is more powerful than You. We are Your servants, and You want us to obey Your rules. Everything about You is real, God. Help me to remember that.

MORNING

## Knowing God's Will

*Do not conform to the pattern of this world, but be transformed by the renewing of your mind. Then you will be able to test and approve what God's will is—his good, pleasing and perfect will.*

Romans 12:2 NIV

Heavenly Father, when You don't answer my prayer right away, I sometimes run on ahead of You. Instead of waiting for Your perfect answer, I do what I want. That can get me into trouble. If I remember to stop and think about what's in Your Word, I'm less likely to make a mistake. Help me, please, to know Your will. I want what You want. Guide me in the right direction. Amen.

EVENING

## In God's Hands

*"Who among all these does not know that the hand of the Lord has done this? In His hand is the life of every living thing and the breath of all men."*

Job 12:9–10 NLV

Lord, I've heard people say, "It's in God's hands." I hadn't thought about that until I read today's verse. Your hands made everything. You are way greater than anything I can imagine. But I can think of Your hands holding the earth. There's nothing on earth You don't know about. You control every breath of every living thing. Our lives depend on You. Your hands are loving and strong. I feel safe in them, Father. Amen.

MORNING

## Trust Your Work to God

*All the ways of a man are pure in his own eyes, but the Lord weighs the thoughts of the heart. Trust your work to the Lord, and your plans will work out well.*

PROVERBS 16:2–3 NLV

Dear Father, this morning I ask that You stop me if I try to do things my way instead of Yours. I know if I trust my work to You, it will turn out well. If my thoughts stray from Your will, rein me in. Set my thoughts in line with Yours. I will do my best to listen to Your voice in my heart. Lead me, Father. Guide me through this day. Amen.

EVENING

## God Cares

*You look over my path and my lying down. You know all my ways very well.*

PSALM 139:3 NLV

Lord, I thank You that You are the God who cares! You want the best for me. You have my life all planned. I'm Your work in progress. Your work in me is powerful, yet gentle and kind. You've planted dreams inside me and given me goals to reach. Help me to put all my faith and trust in You, Father, as You work out Your plan for my life.

# DAY 82

## MORNING

## Helping the Poor

*Blessed be ye poor: for yours is the kingdom of God.*

Luke 6:20 KJV

Jesus, I think I understand what "poor in Spirit" means. It means that we really need to rely on You. I want You to fill me up with You! Help me also to see those who need more, whether that be more of You or more of something else. Open my eyes to their needs. Then let Your Spirit work through me to bless them. Amen.

## EVENING

## God Is My Teacher

*I will instruct you and teach you in the way you should go; I will counsel you with my loving eye on you.*

Psalm 32:8 NIV

Dear God, You are the best teacher ever! You know absolutely everything, and You know the best ways to teach each of Your children. You love us, and You want us to learn Your ways so we can have good lives. We might not be aware, but You are always teaching us and helping us to grow. I want to be a good student, Father. Help me to listen so I can hear Your directions.

MORNING

## Wake UP!

*The Holy Writings say, "Wake up, you who are sleeping. Rise from the dead and Christ will give you light."*

EPHESIANS 5:14 NLV

Jesus, sometimes when I'm bored, my mind wanders and I don't pay attention. I miss important things. It happens in school, and it happens at home too. "Wake up!" my dad says. I don't want to spend all my time daydreaming. Will You help me, please, to stay awake and pay attention? I have a long day ahead, and I need You. I know I can count on You to keep me focused and strong.

EVENING

## I Trust God's Wisdom

*For the LORD gives wisdom; from his mouth come knowledge and understanding.*

PROVERBS 2:6 NIV

Dear God, I trust in Your wisdom. I wish I had more of it. I want to be wise about so many things. I have lots of questions. Some of them You answer for me right away. For others, I need to wait until You are ready to answer. You are happy to teach me, and I'm eager to learn. Help me to grow in knowledge too, God. And help me to understand Your ways. Amen.

## DAY 84

### MORNING

# Dead and Gone

*Jesus said unto him, Let the dead bury their dead:*
*but go thou and preach the kingdom of God.*
LUKE 9:60 KJV

Heavenly Father, help me to let go of the past and look ahead. What went wrong last week, the mean things I said, the sinful things I did—all that is dead and gone because You forgave me. You don't want me dwelling on past mistakes. You will always give me another chance to please You. So help me to accept Your forgiveness. I know You love me and You want me to move on.

### EVENING

# Nothing Is Too Hard for God

*"I am the LORD, the God of all mankind.*
*Is anything too hard for me?"*
JEREMIAH 32:27 NIV

Lord, there are so many obstacles in my way. I need more energy. I need to feel more willing. More than anything, I need to trust You more. Nothing is too difficult for You, Father. You can do anything! Will You please make a way for me to overcome those things that are in my way? Help me to achieve the goals You have set for me. Thank You, God. I praise You. Good night.

MORNING

# A Clean Heart

*Christ did this so He could set the church apart for Himself. He made it clean by the washing of water with the Word.*
EPHESIANS 5:26 NLV

Dear God, my room gets so messy. I do my best to keep it clean, but sometimes I'm just too busy. I guess what's more important is that I have a clean heart, one that tries to please You by staying away from sin and by reading Your Word every day. Please give me a clean heart, Lord. And help me to keep my room a little cleaner too. Amen.

EVENING

# I Trust God's Plan for My Life

*"For I know the plans I have for you," declares the LORD, "plans to prosper you and not to harm you, plans to give you hope and a future."*
JEREMIAH 29:11 NIV

Father, when I think about the future, I feel a little afraid because I don't know what's coming. Remind me that You have a plan for me. Your plan isn't to harm me but to fill me up with hope for what's ahead. Please help me to be excited about and look forward to what You have planned for me. I know You'll be with me every step of the way, and I trust You.

DAY 86

MORNING

## Pray for the Sick

*"Heal the sick. Say to them, 'The holy nation of God is near.'"*
LUKE 10:9 NLV

Dear Jesus, You have power to heal not only bodies but people who are sick in spirit—those who don't know You and are lost in sin. I can be Your helper by praying for the sick. If I know someone who is ill, I will pray for that person using their name. And I'll pray too for *all* the sick people in the world. Lord, please heal them. Amen.

EVENING

## God Is Faithful

*The one who calls you is faithful, and he will do it.*
1 THESSALONIANS 5:24 NIV

Lord God, I thank You that You are faithful. No one else is like You. People let me down sometimes. Friends move away. Things and people change. But I can always count on You because You never change, and You will never leave me. You keep every one of Your promises. You are perfect, and Your love for me is perfect. Lord, I praise You for Your faithfulness.

MORNING

# Live a Pure Life

*You know the guidelines we laid out for you from the Master Jesus. God wants you to live a pure life.*

1 Thessalonians 4:2–3 msg

Jesus, You want me to live a pure life. You are my example of what that means. You never sinned. Everything You did was for Your Father in heaven. I want to be like You. I know I will never be perfect like You are. But I can do my best to learn about You and act like You. Help me to live a pure life, Jesus, a life that honors You. Amen.

EVENING

# Wishes and Dreams

*Going a little farther, he fell with his face to the ground and prayed, "My Father, if it is possible, may this cup be taken from me. Yet not as I will, but as you will."*

Matthew 26:39 niv

Heavenly Father, I'm beginning to understand that what I want might not be in line with what You want for me. It's good to have wishes and dreams about what I'd like to accomplish. But I need to remember that You have a plan for me, and it's even better than what I dream of. God, take all my dreams and wishes. Give me what You want instead. I trust You to guide me.

DAY 88

## MORNING

# Give Thanks

*In every thing give thanks: for this is the will of God.*

1 Thessalonians 5:18 KJV

Dear God, I don't thank You nearly enough for all You have given me. You've blessed me with a home, a family, good food to eat, friends, fun things to do, new things to learn. . . You've given me special talents and a good heart that loves and helps others. I have so much to be thankful for. I'm going to be better at saying, "Thank You, Lord." Thank You for everything!

## EVENING

# I Want to Know You More

*"I want loving-kindness and not a gift to be given in worship. I want people to know God instead of giving burnt gifts."*

Hosea 6:6 NLV

Heavenly Father, I am Your child. I want to know You more. Give me understanding of who You are and what You are like. Teach me the things that are important to You so they can become important to me too. Help me to always put You first in my life. Give me wisdom to choose time spent with You over distractions that keep me too busy for You. Amen.

MORNING

## Words, Words, Words

*As new babies want milk, you should want to drink the pure milk which is God's Word so you will grow up and be saved from the punishment of sin. If you have tasted of the Lord, you know how good He is.*

1 Peter 2:2–3 NLV

Father, my life is so full of words. I'm learning new words every day! I know some words that You don't approve of. I hear them all around me. I want all my words to glorify You. As I read the Bible, I'm learning what pleases You. Pleasant, respectful words are like music to Your ears. Let my words always honor You. Amen.

EVENING

## The One True God

*We know God's Son has come. He has given us the understanding to know Him Who is the true God. We are joined together with the true God through His Son, Jesus Christ. He is the true God and the life that lasts forever.*

1 John 5:20 NLV

Dear God, You are the one true God. The only real God. We are joined together with You through Your Son, Jesus. He is the only true Son of God. He walked here on earth, died for our sins, arose from the dead, and returned to You in heaven. You and Jesus are forever. That is the absolute truth, and I believe it. Amen.

MORNING

## Delight to Do God's Will

*I delight to do thy will, O my God.*

PSALM 40:8 KJV

Dear heavenly Father, You are a good Father who gives good gifts to His children. You pour Your love over me and bless me in so many ways. I know that Your will—what You want for me—is perfect. Help me to listen for Your voice in my heart and to do Your will. As You bless me, I am delighted to pass Your blessings on to others. Please show me how.

EVENING

## I'm So Emotional!

*"The LORD is slow to anger, abounding in love and forgiving sin and rebellion."*

NUMBERS 14:18 NIV

God, my emotions are all over the place! Sometimes I'm so happy. Other times I feel like crying. I can quickly fall in love with something (or someone) and then fall out of love just as fast. I get angry, and I can be stubborn. God, help me to be more like You. The Bible says You are slow to anger, overflowing in love, and always ready to forgive. That's how I want to be.

MORNING

## God Heals the Brokenhearted

*He heals the brokenhearted and binds up their wounds.*

PSALM 147:3 NASB

Oh Father, my heart is broken. I don't have to tell You why. You already know. I'm coming to You for comfort in this quiet time we have together. Pour out Your love to me. Remind me that there is nothing You can't do. Dry my tears and heal my heart. I know You have this situation in Your control, and You will work it out for my good. I love You, Lord. Amen.

EVENING

## Let Us Love One Another

*Dear friends, let us love one another, for love comes from God. Everyone who loves has been born of God and knows God.*

1 JOHN 4:7 NIV

Dear Lord, as I read Your Word and discover what love really is, help me express that love for others. You are so good at loving people—You are kind, caring, interested, accepting, and forgiving. You seek the best for others. You understand everyone's emotions, what makes them happy and what makes them sad. You make people feel special. Lord, let me be a person who loves like that. Amen.

DAY 92

MORNING

# Forever

*The world and all its desires will pass away. But the man who obeys God and does what He wants done will live forever.*

1 JOHN 2:17 NLV

Jesus, when I have a problem, I think it's never going to end. But You are the great problem solver. With Your help, problems always get solved one way or another. Whatever I worry about, whatever I want—everything comes to an end. Nothing on earth lasts forever. When I leave earth one day, I have the promise of forever life with You in heaven. You are forever, Jesus, and I'm grateful for You. Amen.

EVENING

# I Will Be Patient

*Be patient, then, brothers and sisters, until the Lord's coming. See how the farmer waits for the land to yield its valuable crop, patiently waiting for the autumn and spring rains.*

JAMES 5:7 NIV

Heavenly Father, waiting is hard. There are so many things I want right away. I know You will answer my prayers in Your time, according to Your will and not mine. You know what's best for me. I ask for the willingness and courage to wait until You are ready. I ask You to help me trust You in the meantime. I will do my best, Lord, to wait patiently. Amen.

MORNING

# First Things First

*But seek ye first the kingdom of God, and his righteousness; and all these things shall be added unto you.*

MATTHEW 6:33 KJV

Dear God, You understand all the stuff I have to do. There's homework, chores at home, activities after school, promises to keep, pets to care for. . . These things are important, but they aren't more important than the time I spend with You. Remind me to always put You ahead of everything else. If I do that, You will take care of all the other things I have going on in my life.

EVENING

# Confidence

*Do not be afraid of fear that comes all at once. And do not be afraid of the storm of the sinful when it comes. For the Lord will be your trust. He will keep your foot from being caught.*

PROVERBS 3:25–26 NLV

Lord, I want to be more confident—more willing to put all my trust in You. I have faith that if trouble comes, You will bring me through it. You are bigger and more powerful than anything! I don't have to be afraid. Even if I mess up, You have the power to make things right again. Thank You for the confidence You give me. Help me to have even more. Amen.

MORNING

## Joy School

*"Come to Me, all who are weary and burdened, and I will give you rest. Take My yoke upon you and learn from Me, for I am gentle and humble in heart, and you will find rest for your souls."*

MATTHEW 11:28–29 NASB

Dear Jesus, instead of going to school this morning, I wish I could go to "joy school." I'm crabby. I'd rather stay home. But the Bible says that when I feel this way, I should come to You. I know You will help me to have a better attitude. Please take my crabbiness away and show me how to find some joy. Help me to act more like You. Amen.

EVENING

## Stress

*Cast your cares on the LORD and he will sustain you; he will never let the righteous be shaken.*

PSALM 55:22 NIV

Father God, sometimes my life is. . .well, I guess it's just too much! I get stressed out. When that happens, even the smallest problems seem big. I give You all my cares and worries tonight. Take them and work on them for me. I don't have to be stressed if I remember that You are the one in control. Help me to relax and sleep well. I will fall asleep remembering that You love me.

MORNING

## Amazing Forgiveness

*Because of the blood of Christ, we are bought and made free from the punishment of sin. And because of His blood, our sins are forgiven. His loving-favor to us is so rich.*

EPHESIANS 1:7 NLV

Lord, I don't thank You often enough for Your gift of forgiveness. It's amazing that You allowed Your body to suffer on the cross because of Your love for me. You took the sins of the world on Yourself and were punished for them so I wouldn't be. Because of Your gift of forgiveness, I get to live forever with You in heaven one day. Thank You, dear Jesus! Amen.

EVENING

## My Companion

*"Surely I am with you always, to the very end of the age."*

MATTHEW 28:20 NIV

Dear God, I thank You that You are my true companion—that I am never alone. You have assigned angels to watch over and protect me. You are with me always—all the days of my life here on earth and then forever in heaven. You are my all-the-time companion, my best friend. I enjoy our friendship, God! Help me to always be a good friend to You.

# DAY 96

## MORNING

# I Won't Give Up

*You must be willing to wait without giving up. After you have done what God wants you to do, God will give you what He promised you.*

HEBREWS 10:36 NLV

Heavenly Father, You keep whispering in my heart, "Be patient. It will take time." But waiting is still so hard for me. I want the time to be *now*. When I become impatient, I start to doubt You, and I don't want to do that. Lord, I will never give up on You. I know You will answer my prayers. Help me to keep going, trusting in You. I know You always keep Your promises.

## EVENING

# I Messed Up

*I said, "I will tell my sins to the Lord."*
*And You forgave the guilt of my sin.*

PSALM 32:5 NLV

Father, I feel guilty because I messed up and I knew better. I've come to tell You all about it. You know everything I've done wrong; yet when I come to say "I'm sorry," You are ready to forgive me. I never have to worry that You will hold my sins against me. You are gentle toward me. You always treat me with caring and love. Thank You, God. Amen.

MORNING

## New Each Day

*Therefore, if anyone is in Christ, the new creation has come: The old has gone, the new is here!*

2 Corinthians 5:17 niv

Father, You make each day special. I have so many new things to discover, not just about the world but about myself too. Every day I learn a little more about You and how You want me to live. You help me let go of the not-so-good habits I have and replace them with others that please You. You replace old experiences I've outgrown with new ones. Thank You, God, for each new day.

EVENING

## A New Song

*He put a new song in my mouth,*
*a hymn of praise to our God.*

Psalm 40:3 niv

Lord, give me a new song to sing, a happier tune! I've been complaining a lot lately. I know there's no mess too big for You to fix. If I feel like complaining, give me positive words to say instead. If I feel like pouting, give me something to laugh about. My heart should be happy all the time because You are my God, my protector, and my best friend. Father, I praise You!

MORNING

# God Gives Me Enough

*God can give you all you need. He will give you more than enough. You will have everything you need for yourselves. And you will have enough left over to give when there is a need.*

2 CORINTHIANS 9:8 NLV

Dear Lord, whatever I have right now, it's enough. You know exactly what I need every minute of each day. I might not think it's enough, but You do. If You hold something back that I want, You have a perfect reason for making me wait. You are enough for me, God. I trust You to supply all my needs at the perfect time and in line with Your will. Amen.

EVENING

# Thank You for Jesus!

*For God so loved the world that he gave his one and only Son, that whoever believes in him shall not perish but have eternal life.*

JOHN 3:16 NIV

Father, You gave me the most precious gift, Your very own Son, so I could live forever with You in heaven. How it must have hurt You to see Jesus suffer. But I know You allowed Him to go through all that suffering because You love me. Jesus was willing to give His life for mine. That kind of love is more than I can imagine. Thank You, God, for Jesus!

MORNING

## God Provides What I Need

*You open Your hand and satisfy the desire of every living thing.*

PSALM 145:16 NKJV

Dear God, there's no creature on earth You don't provide for. The Bible says that if even one sparrow falls to earth, You know about it. You see every living thing and provide for its needs. I praise You right now for the daily things You supply for me. Help me to always be thankful for what I have. Your power is awesome. Thank You for giving me what I need every day.

EVENING

## Follow Jesus

*Then he said to the crowd, "If any of you wants to be my follower, you must give up your own way, take up your cross daily, and follow me."*

LUKE 9:23 NLT

Jesus, You gave up so much for me when You died on the cross. All You ask of me is to follow You. That means learning as much as I can about You and the things You taught us when You lived here on earth. I want to give up everything that isn't pleasing to God and become more like You. I'm listening, Jesus. I'm ready to follow You. Let's go!

DAY 100

MORNING

## Quiet Time with God

*For in six days the Lord made the heavens, the earth, the sea and all that is in them. And He rested on the seventh day. So the Lord gave honor to the Day of Rest and made it holy.*

EXODUS 20:11 NLV

Dear heavenly Father, the Bible says after You made everything in the sky and on earth, You rested. You never get tired, so that wasn't the reason You needed rest. Maybe You just wanted to spend quiet time looking at all the wonderful things You had made. The time we spend together is my quiet time. I rest with You, talking with You. Quiet time with You is the best part of my day.

EVENING

## God Is My Helper

*See, God is my Helper. The Lord is the One Who keeps my soul alive.*

PSALM 54:4 NLV

Dear God, sometimes I think I should work out my problems on my own. I don't want to bother You with what's bothering me. But then I remember that You want to be my helper. You are just waiting for me to ask, so I'm asking—please, help. You know what's going on. Forgive me for not coming to You sooner. Please show me what to do. Amen.

MORNING

## God's Riches

*And my God will give you everything you need because of His great riches in Christ Jesus.*

PHILIPPIANS 4:19 NLV

Father, when I hear the word *riches*, I think of having everything my heart desires—cool shoes and clothes, money to spend any way I want, maybe even a big swimming pool! But that's not what You mean by "riches." The Bible says Jesus is everything I should want and need. True riches are things like His love, forgiveness, and the many ways He helps me each day. Thank You for reminding me, God. Amen.

EVENING

## My Faith Gives Me Strength

*Just as you received Christ Jesus as Lord, continue to live your lives in him, rooted and built up in him, strengthened in the faith as you were taught, and overflowing with thankfulness.*

COLOSSIANS 2:6–7 NIV

Lord, my faith in You makes me strong. Thank You for always being with me. I'm grateful for the help You give me. You boost my confidence to try new things and keep trying. If I fail, You pick me up, comfort me, and teach me how to do better next time. What would I ever do without You! I'm so thankful for You. Jesus, You are the one I'm sure I can count on.

# DAY 102

## MORNING

# Remember to Pray for Others

*The Lord thunders in front of His army. His army has too many to number. Those who obey His Word are powerful.*

JOEL 2:11 NLV

Dear Lord, I'm pretty good at noticing when others need help. I tell myself to pray for them, but sometimes I forget. Those who believe in You are like a huge army. When we pray, our words are powerful. They reach our commander—*You*! And You will surely answer our prayers. Remind me, God, that You command me to pray for others. Help me to help them by reaching out to You in prayer. Amen.

## EVENING

# My Shepherd

*The LORD is my shepherd; I shall not want.*

PSALM 23:1 KJV

A good shepherd takes good care of his sheep. He never lets them out of his sight. He watches out for predators and protects his flock. He knows each sheep by name, and he makes sure each has everything it needs. You are that kind of shepherd, Lord. You watch over us, protecting us, loving us, and providing for our every need. I'm grateful to be one of Your "sheep." You are everything I want. Amen.

MORNING

## Open My Eyes, Lord

*I pray that your hearts will be able to understand. I pray that you will know about the hope given by God's call. I pray that you will see how great the things are that He has promised to those who belong to Him. I pray that you will know how great His power is for those who have put their trust in Him.*

EPHESIANS 1:18–19 NLV

Father, thank You for this new day. This morning, open the eyes of my heart so I will understand what You want me to do. Fill me with Your amazing power. Give me hope that today is going to be a great day. Guide me in all that I do, and remind me to put my trust in You. Amen.

EVENING

## God Is My Strength

*"God is my strength and power,*
*and He makes my way perfect."*

2 SAMUEL 22:33 NKJV

Dear heavenly Father, it's been a long day, and I'm tired. Please recharge my soul with Your strength. Help me to sleep well tonight so I'll be ready for tomorrow. I sometimes make things harder on myself because I try to handle them all on my own. Remind me that my help comes from You—You are ready to supply whatever I need. Your way is perfect. Thank You, God. Amen.

MORNING

# A Morning Prayer

*The Sovereign LORD has given me his words of wisdom, so that I know how to comfort the weary. Morning by morning he wakens me and opens my understanding to his will.*

ISAIAH 50:4 NLT

Father God, You give me strength when I'm tired and overwhelmed. You know how to comfort me and give me hope. This morning I pray, asking You to show me how to help my friends find comfort and hope in You. I want to use the strength You've given me to be their helper. Give me wisdom and the words to share You with them, Lord. Guide them to find comfort in You. Amen.

EVENING

# An Evening Prayer

*"No one is holy like the LORD, for there is none besides You, nor is there any rock like our God."*

1 SAMUEL 2:2 NKJV

Oh God, there is no one like You. Everything about You is perfect. Nothing is a match for Your amazing power. You rule the universe! You are all things good, never selfish, always giving. You share all that You are with me and guide me to living a life that honors You. You are the one true God—*my* God! I praise You, and I love You. Amen.

MORNING

## Right There with Me

*I will praise the LORD, who counsels me;*
*even at night my heart instructs me.*
PSALM 16:7 NIV

Dear God, sometimes I go to sleep worried about a problem, and when I wake in the morning, the answer is there in my head. It seems to have appeared as I slept. That came from You, Lord. You speak to my heart even when I am asleep and not aware. I'm comforted to know that You are right there with me all the time, even when I'm sleeping. Amen.

EVENING

## I Made a Mistake

*Indeed, we all make many mistakes. For if we could control our tongues, we would be perfect and could also control ourselves in every other way.*
JAMES 3:2 NLT

Oh God, I made a mistake. I really messed up this time. I didn't think before I opened my mouth, and I said something I shouldn't have. Now my best friend is upset with me. What can I do to make things right? Give me courage to admit to her that what I said was wrong. Please help us to be friends again. And God, give me wisdom to do better next time.

## DAY 106

MORNING

# Look at the Birds

*"Look at the birds. They do not plant seeds. They do not gather grain. They have no grain buildings for keeping grain. Yet God feeds them. Are you not worth more than the birds?"*

LUKE 12:24 NLV

God, if You keep track of the lives of birds, then I know I can trust You to watch over me. You are always looking after me. And although You love and care for the animals, You say I'm even more important to You. Your love has no boundaries. You love me all the time, no matter what! I know I don't deserve that. I thank You, God, for taking such good care of me.

EVENING

# Mountains Out of Molehills

*"I tell you this: Do not worry about your life. Do not worry about what you are going to eat and drink. Do not worry about what you are going to wear. Is not life more important than food? Is not the body more important than clothes?"*

MATTHEW 6:25 NLV

Heavenly Father, my grandpa likes to say, "Don't make mountains out of molehills." He says it means don't worry so much about the little stuff. Today's Bible verse reminds me of that. You have everything—all the little stuff and the big stuff—under control. My job is to give my worries to You when I pray and then trust You to work things out. Thanks for the reminder, God.

MORNING

## You and I Together

*[Jesus said,] "The Spirit alone gives eternal life. Human effort accomplishes nothing. And the very words I have spoken to you are spirit and life."*

JOHN 6:63 NLT

Jesus, sometimes I try and try yet still accomplish nothing. I so often forget to come to You first. I need Your strength giving me power; otherwise, my efforts are useless. Guide me through Your Word. Remind me of the things You say in the Bible. Speak to my heart with Your gentle voice. Calm me and remind me that You and I do everything together. Amen.

EVENING

## Control Your Tongue

*If you claim to be religious but don't control your tongue, you are fooling yourself, and your religion is worthless.*

JAMES 1:26 NLT

Father, I want You to be pleased with the language I use, but sometimes my tongue seems to have a mind of its own. I don't always think before I speak, and I say things I shouldn't. My words can hurt someone's feelings. They can show disrespect for my parents, other adults, and worst of all, You. I want my words to bring others nearer to You. Please help me to choose my words wisely.

DAY 108

MORNING

## The Bible Is My Guide

*All Scripture is God-breathed and is useful for teaching, rebuking, correcting and training in righteousness.*

2 Timothy 3:16 niv

Dear heavenly Father, Your Word, the Bible, has everything I need. It teaches me, comforts me, corrects me, and gives me strength. The words in the Bible are Your words speaking to me. The Bible teaches me about You and helps me learn the kinds of behavior You expect from me. The Bible is my guidebook. If I follow its instructions, it will lead me through life.

EVENING

## Three Steps to Good Speech

*Everyone should be quick to listen, slow to speak and slow to become angry.*

James 1:19 niv

Dear God, there are certain steps to follow when learning something new. The Bible offers three steps to help me when I'm talking with others. Step one: Listen to what others are saying before I speak. Step two: Pray before I say something I might end up being sorry for. Step three: Don't speak if I'm angry. Help me, Lord, to remember these steps every day.

MORNING

## God Knows What I Need

*Do not worry. Learn to pray about everything. Give thanks to God as you ask Him for what you need.*

PHILIPPIANS 4:6 NLV

Even while I'm asking You for something, Lord, I can already thank You. I know You hear my prayers and will answer with "Yes," "No," or "Wait." Thank You for taking care of my needs even before I ask. You already know what I need before I come to You. I'm sure I can trust You to answer me in the best way and according to Your purpose. Thank You, God. Amen.

EVENING

## Safe in Danger

*For in the day of trouble he will keep me safe in his dwelling; he will hide me in the shelter of his sacred tent and set me high upon a rock.*

PSALM 27:5 NIV

Dear heavenly Father, when I was little, I was afraid of many things. But then I learned that I can always trust You. Now whenever I'm afraid, I remember that You protect me. Your love is like a warm blanket wrapped around me, comforting me. I am safe with You whether I'm afraid of a tiny, stinging bug or a big, rumbling storm. You are always with me, keeping me out of harm's way.

DAY 110

MORNING

# Different Gifts

*There are different kinds of gifts, but the same Spirit.*

1 Corinthians 12:4 niv

Dear God, You give each of us different gifts, things we are good at. I'm good at dancing and singing and a few other things. My best friend is good at drawing. My mom is the best cook, and my dad likes to build things. He's good at figuring things out. I'm glad You gave us different skills and talents. It's interesting to see what each of us can do and to learn from one another.

EVENING

# Never Alone

*"I will never leave you nor forsake you."*

Joshua 1:5 niv

Jesus, my Lord and my friend, You say You will never leave me. Still, sometimes I feel lonely. I need to remember that even when I don't feel You with me, You are right here. You are more than a feeling. I know in my heart that You exist. You promise to stay with me, protect me, and love me. Please help me to feel less alone. Lift my spirits and fill me with joy.

MORNING

## Always-Listening Ears

*If we are sure He hears us when we ask,*
*we can be sure He will give us what we ask for.*

1 John 5:15 NLV

Thank You, God, that You are always listening to me. You never ignore my prayers, no matter how silly or unimportant I think my words might be. It's a mystery how You can possibly hear the requests of all the people on earth at the same time, but You do! And each moment of those prayers is important to You. Thank You for being a God with always-listening ears. Amen.

EVENING

## God Takes Away My Fears

*I looked for the Lord, and He answered me.*
*And He took away all my fears.*

Psalm 34:4 NLV

Dear God, when I'm afraid, I feel kind of frozen. I don't know what to do. I usually forget I should look for You. I will find You in the Bible and inside my heart. You haven't left me. Help me to trust in You more. Remind me, whenever I'm afraid, that You are my courage and my strength. You are the one who takes away all my fears. Amen.

DAY 112

MORNING

# A Work in Progress

*And we know that all things work together for good to them that love God, to them who are the called according to his purpose.*

ROMANS 8:28 KJV

Lord, my life is like one gigantic jigsaw puzzle. Little by little, You are putting it together. Many of the pieces are hidden from me, but You know where they are. As You put together the puzzle that's my life, You are working everything out for my good. The last piece of the puzzle is the day I meet You in heaven. I won't be finished until then. I am a work in progress. Amen.

EVENING

# No Doubt

*But when you ask, you must believe and not doubt, because the one who doubts is like a wave of the sea, blown and tossed by the wind.*

JAMES 1:6 NIV

Heavenly Father, doubt is like being in a small boat on a stormy sea. Doubt makes me feel like I'm wildly rocking back and forth, tipping this way and that. Help me to believe You will take care of me. If I trust in You, I know You will guide me on the right path. I can do almost anything I set my mind to, if only I trust in You. Amen.

MORNING

## I Will Not Be Afraid

*So we say with confidence, "The Lord is my helper; I will not be afraid. What can mere mortals do to me?"*

HEBREWS 13:6 NIV

Dear God, whenever I have to face trouble or something big and challenging, I remember that You are my helper. I say to myself, "God is with me. I will not be afraid!" Then I trust You to be right there to meet whatever gets in my way. You are bigger and much more powerful than anything on earth—and You are my protector. I'm safe with You. Amen.

EVENING

## Keeping His Commands

*Whatsoever we ask, we receive of him, because we keep his commandments, and do those things that are pleasing in his sight.*

1 JOHN 3:22 KJV

Father God, I know the Ten Commandments, but I don't always keep them. I'm sorry to say that I don't hold them in my mind all day long. Help me to remember Your commandments and always live in a way that pleases You. Your commandments aren't meant to make life hard for me; they're instead meant to protect me from harm and lead me nearer to You. Forgive me for not following them. Amen.

DAY 114

MORNING

# God's Faithfulness Is Forever

*Your faithfulness endures to all generations.*

Psalm 119:90 NKJV

Dear God, Your Word, the Bible, is ancient. It was written long, long ago, but its words are just as true today as they were then. Its instructions are for me, my parents, my grandparents, my great-grandparents—all the way back through the generations. You have loved and been faithful to everyone who has ever lived, and Your love and faithfulness will last forever.

EVENING

# God's Word Gives Me Confidence

*For You are my hope, O Lord God.*
*You are my trust since I was young.*

Psalm 71:5 NLV

Father, even before I was old enough to know who You are, people prayed for me. They hoped I would accept You as my God and learn to love and trust You. Now that I'm older, I'm learning more about You every day. The Bible helps with that. It gives me confidence that You are always with me and that You love me. It gives me hope that I can always count on Your promises.

MORNING

## Keep Asking

*Ask, and it shall be given you; seek, and ye shall find; knock, and it shall be opened unto you.*

MATTHEW 7:7 KJV

Dear Father God, there are many things I don't understand about You—like why You don't answer my prayers right away. The Bible says You want us to keep coming to You and to keep asking until we get an answer. Maybe that brings us nearer to You. Your timing is always perfect. So when You don't answer me right away, I will keep asking and seeking Your will. Amen.

EVENING

## God's Love Is Perfect

*There is no fear in love. Perfect love puts fear out of our hearts. People have fear when they are afraid of being punished. The man who is afraid does not have perfect love.*

1 JOHN 4:18 NLV

Lord, help me to trust more in Your love. I'm afraid sometimes of being punished or being left alone. I know I don't have to be afraid of anything, because Your love is all around me. I might not feel it, but it's there. You love me with a perfect love, a love that is all-the-time powerful and strong, a love that is far bigger and stronger than anything that makes me afraid.

DAY 116

MORNING

## God Helps Me Understand

*The opening up of Your Word gives light.*
*It gives understanding to the child-like.*
PSALM 119:130 NLV

Heavenly Father, the words in the Bible can be hard to understand. When I don't understand Your Word, I know You will help me. I'm grateful for people in my life who can explain some of the scripture verses. My parents and grandparents help, and so do my older siblings and my pastor. If I have questions, I'm not afraid to ask, because I want to learn all about You.

EVENING

## God Makes Me Strong

*"Do not fear, for I am with you; do not be dismayed,*
*for I am your God. I will strengthen you and help you;*
*I will uphold you with my righteous right hand."*
ISAIAH 41:10 NIV

Dear God, when I hear the word *strength*, I think of a strong body. But the Bible teaches a different kind of strength. Strength is part of my character—what makes me who I am inside. When I feel brave, that's You giving me strength. If I keep trying after I fail, that's You giving me strength too. Your kind of strength gives me confidence; and with Your help, I can do almost anything! Amen.

MORNING

## Prayer Time

*Therefore I say unto you, What things soever ye desire, when ye pray, believe that ye receive them, and ye shall have them.*
MARK 11:24 KJV

Thank You, God, for sharing this time of prayer with me. Who am I that You—God!—want to spend time with me? But You do. When I ask for something in prayer, I don't want to be selfish. I want what You want for me. And I trust that You will give me whatever I truly need. Father, I'm grateful that You welcome me to come to You in prayer. Amen.

EVENING

## Joy in Giving

*Each of you should give what you have decided in your heart to give, not reluctantly or under compulsion, for God loves a cheerful giver.*
2 CORINTHIANS 9:7 NIV

Lord Jesus, open my eyes to the many ways I can give to others. I want to be a cheerful giver. Whether I'm giving my time or my help, or even giving away something to someone who needs it more than I do, I want to give willingly and without complaining. Please show me how I can help, and then let my giving be a blessing to others. Amen.

MORNING

# Jesus Loves Kids!

*[Jesus] took the children in his arms,*
*placed his hands on them and blessed them.*

Mark 10:16 NIV

Jesus, a crowd of grown-ups were wanting Your attention, but as soon as You saw kids, You took them in Your arms, placed Your hands on their heads, and blessed them. You must really love kids, Jesus. I know You always have time for me. You are with me wherever I go, guiding and protecting me. You celebrate all my accomplishments. I know You love me, and I love You too. Amen.

EVENING

# Whatever I Need

*"Look at the birds of the air; they do not sow or reap or store away in barns, and yet your heavenly Father feeds them. Are you not much more valuable than they? Can any one of you by worrying add a single hour to your life?"*

Matthew 6:26–27 NIV

Father God, I know You will provide whatever I need. Whether it's comfort or confidence, food or fun, You'll see that I have it. If I need a friend, You'll find one for me. When I need help, I'm sure You will send someone—maybe even one of Your angels—to be with me and protect me. You, Father, promise to meet all my needs, and I trust You. Amen.

MORNING

## Tomorrow

*"Do not worry about tomorrow. Tomorrow will have its own worries. The troubles we have in a day are enough for one day."*

MATTHEW 6:34 NLV

Dear Jesus, You already know that tomorrow is a very big day for me. I'm really getting nervous, because I don't know how everything will turn out. But *You* do! You have tomorrow all planned for me, every minute of it. I don't have to worry about tomorrow, because You have it in Your control. So, Jesus, I'm just going to set my thoughts on today. Let's go and make it a good one! Amen.

EVENING

## Thank You for My Friends

*One who has unreliable friends soon comes to ruin, but there is a friend who sticks closer than a brother.*

PROVERBS 18:24 NIV

Father, thank You for my friends! I'm grateful for each one. They have different ways of bringing fun into my life. Some are good listeners; others know just what to say when I'm feeling sad. They all have different things they're good at, and I learn from them. I enjoy playing with them and hanging out. You are the giver of all good gifts, and I thank You, Lord, for the gift of my friends.

MORNING

# Heart's Desire

*Be happy in the Lord. And He will give you the desires of your heart.*

PSALM 37:4 NLV

Dear Lord, the desires of my heart change almost every day. I want one thing. Then that want fades away, and I want something else. Maybe what I want isn't really what I need. When I ask You to meet my needs, I know You will give me Your best. And Your best will make me happy. Put inside my heart whatever You desire. Help me to line up my thoughts with Yours. Amen.

EVENING

# Make Me a Better Listener

*Come and hear, all you who fear God; let me tell you what he has done for me.*

PSALM 66:16 NIV

Dear heavenly Father, I'm not always a good listener. I daydream sometimes when my teacher is speaking, and I don't always listen carefully when my parents give me instructions. Sometimes I get ahead of whoever is speaking, and I want to jump right in and say my own words. Lord, help me to become a better listener, and help me especially to listen to You when You speak to my heart. Amen.

MORNING

## Let It Go

*As far as the east is from the west, so far has*
*He removed our transgressions from us.*

PSALM 103:12 NKJV

Dear God, last week I did something I'm not proud of. I've been upset with myself ever since. I knew what I did was wrong, but I did it anyway. You've forgiven me—like You always do— but I haven't forgiven myself. Please help me to let it go. You know I'm sorry and I'll try harder next time. I need to forgive myself now and feel happy again. Amen.

EVENING

## Jesus' Kind of Love

*[Jesus said,] "Love one another; as I have loved you."*

JOHN 13:34 NKJV

Jesus, You are the best example of love. You cared for people, feeding them and healing them when they were sick and hurt. You welcomed huge crowds of Your followers even when You were tired. You always had time for children. You taught about forgiveness and God's love. You loved us so much that You died for us so we could live with You someday in heaven. Help me to love with Your kind of love.

MORNING

## Open Your Heart

*I am the LORD thy God, which brought thee out of the land of Egypt: open thy mouth wide, and I will fill it.*

PSALM 81:10 KJV

Dear God, today's Bible verse makes me think of a baby bird opening its mouth wide, waiting for its mom to feed it. I think that's how You want us to open our hearts to You. If we open our hearts, You will fill them with Your love, wisdom, and power. I want more of You, Lord. Here is my heart wide open. Fill it up, please. Feed me with Your goodness and love. Amen.

EVENING

## I Pray for My Friends

*The LORD also restored the fortunes of Job when he prayed for his friends, and the LORD increased double all that Job had.*

JOB 42:10 NASB

Dear heavenly Father, thank You for reminding me to pray for my friends. I can pray for them when they are sick or unhappy. I can pray if they are worried or afraid. Most important, I can pray for them to know You. There are so many reasons to pray for my friends. Even if they hurt or disappoint me, I should pray for them. Everyone needs prayers. Amen.

MORNING

## A New Heaven and Earth

*Now I saw a new heaven and a new earth, for the first heaven and the first earth had passed away.*

REVELATION 21:1 NKJV

Father God, some parts of the Bible are hard to understand, especially parts that talk about things that will happen far into the future. Someday Jesus will come back to earth again. Someday You will create a new earth and a new heaven, and earth will be perfect—as perfect as You made it to be before it got messed up by sin. I wonder, Father, when will it happen? No one knows. Amen.

EVENING

## Wisdom Is Sweet, Like Honey

*Know also that wisdom is like honey for you: If you find it, there is a future hope for you, and your hope will not be cut off.*

PROVERBS 24:14 NIV

Dear God, I love it when You help me discover something new that I've never realized before. That's what happens when I spend time reading my Bible and thinking about what it says. You open my eyes to see something new, and I want to put it into practice and share what I've found with others. Thanks to You, I've made some sweet discoveries. I wonder where they will lead me.

DAY 124

MORNING

## Jesus Will Lead Me

*"The Lord will always lead you. He will meet the needs of your soul in the dry times and give strength to your body. You will be like a garden that has enough water, like a well of water that never dries up."*

ISAIAH 58:11 NLV

Jesus, I can always trust You to lead me. You are with me all the time, and You never give up on me. Even if I take the wrong way in life, You will be beside me, trying to get me back on the right path. Wherever I go and whatever I do, I know You will meet my needs. Thank You, Jesus, for being my very best friend. Amen.

EVENING

## Nothing Can Take Away God's Love

*I am convinced that neither death nor life, neither angels nor demons, neither the present nor the future, nor any powers, neither height nor depth, nor anything else in all creation, will be able to separate us from the love of God that is in Christ Jesus our Lord.*

ROMANS 8:38–39 NIV

Dear God, tonight's Bible verse is a reminder of how much You love me. Nothing can take Your love from me. Hard things now or in the future cannot; people in power cannot. No living thing can take away Your love. Not angels or even death! Because You live in my heart forever, Your love is always with me.

MORNING

## Jesus, I Need You

*For He fills the thirsty soul. And He fills the hungry soul with good things.*

PSALM 107:9 NLV

Jesus, sometimes You feel far away. The problem isn't with You; it's with me. I haven't spent much time with You lately, and my mind has been on other things. My heart—my soul—misses You. It's sort of like when I feel really hungry or thirsty. I want You right away so I will feel better. Come, Lord Jesus. I need You. Fill me up with Your love. Amen.

EVENING

## What If?

*If no one knows what will happen, who can tell him when it will happen?*

ECCLESIASTES 8:7 NLV

God, I'm a worrier. I think about all the what-ifs. What if I fail? What if I don't like the new experience I'm about to have? What if I get hurt? What if I die or if someone I love dies? You are the only one who knows what will happen. The future is in Your hands. Because I know that, I can relax. You love me. You are my protector. I will be okay.

MORNING

## All Day Long

*To declare Your lovingkindness in the morning, and Your faithfulness every night.*

PSALM 92:2 NKJV

Heavenly Father, from morning, all through the day and all through the night, You stay with me. Do You ever get tired of leading me around? I don't think so. I feel You with me all the time. If I need help, You are there. If I have to be brave, You give me strength. When I rest, You spend quiet time with me. Thank You, God, for being my all-the-time friend. Amen.

EVENING

## A Special Kind of Teacher

*"I am the Lord your God, Who teaches you to do well, Who leads you in the way you should go."*

ISAIAH 48:17 NLV

God, You are a special kind of teacher. You don't teach me reading or math or science. You give that job to my teachers in school. You teach me how to live right. If I read the Bible, learn what You expect from me, and live to please You, then I will do well in life. I'm learning from You, God. But I have so much more to learn. Continue to teach me. Amen.

MORNING

## From Parent to Child

*"Know then that the Lord your God is God, the faithful God. He keeps His promise and shows His loving-kindness to those who love Him and keep His Laws, even to a thousand family groups in the future."*

DEUTERONOMY 7:9 NLV

God, thank You for the people in my family who teach me about You. It's important for parents to tell their children about You. When they grow up, their children will tell their children, who will tell their children—and on and on. From that day when You put Adam and Eve, the first man and woman, on earth, parents have been telling their kids about You. They will do that forever.

EVENING

## God's Plans Are Forever

*But the plans of the LORD stand firm forever, the purposes of his heart through all generations.*

PSALM 33:11 NIV

Father, You never change Your plans, because everything You do is perfect. When You make a plan, it's perfectly complete. When You created me, You planned my whole life. But not just my life, Lord! You know if I'll have children one day. You already have their lives planned, and on and on. You know who my grandchildren will be and my great-grandchildren. You have everything on earth all planned out forever. That's so amazing!

MORNING

## Redemption

*In [Jesus Christ] we have redemption through his blood, the forgiveness of sins, according to the riches of his grace.*

EPHESIANS 1:7 KJV

Lord, I looked up that word *redemption*. It means "to be set free from sin." When Jesus died on the cross, my sins (past, present, and future) died with Him. I was set free from them because Jesus took the punishment for me. Because of Him, I don't have to worry that You won't forgive me when I displease You. I have Your forgiveness forever. My heart is made clean so You can come in.

EVENING

## Good Health

*"Say to [Nabal]: 'Long life to you! Good health to you and your household! And good health to all that is yours!'"*

1 SAMUEL 25:6 NIV

Dear God, You made my body, and it's my job to take care of it. I do that by eating healthy, drinking enough water, and exercising every day. I don't always remember to do those things. I want to do better. Help me to make wise choices about my health so I might live a long and healthy life. Please keep me from getting hurt or sick, and keep me safe. Amen.

MORNING

## God, I Praise You!

*He dawns on them like the morning light when the sun rises on a cloudless morning, when the tender grass springs out of the earth through clear shining after rain.*

2 Samuel 23:4 ampc

Lord, I praise You for the beauty of the earth, for its fiery sunrises followed by blue skies and starry nights. I praise You for green grass, flowers and fields, mountains and hills. I praise You for Your power that created it all. There are so many wonderful reasons to praise You, Lord. When I praise You, I feel different: filled with joy. I feel like a plant washed clean after a spring rain. Amen.

EVENING

## God Cares for Me

*Cast all your anxiety on him because he cares for you.*

1 Peter 5:7 niv

Dear God, I feel calm when I give You my problems. When I'm troubled or afraid, I can stop worrying and relax because You care for me. You give me strength to stand up to anything that gets in my way. You are more powerful than anything that can hurt me. If I need to make a big decision, You can help with that too. You love me and take good care of me.

MORNING

## A New Way

*"This is My blood of the New Way of Worship which is given for many. It is given so the sins of many can be forgiven."*

MATTHEW 26:28 NLV

Jesus, before God sent You to earth, His people had many rules to follow. They brought gifts and offered them to God for their sins to be forgiven so they could get to heaven. But when God sent You, You took all their sins away. You came so that whenever people messed up, God would forgive them anyway. You made a way to heaven for all who trust in You. Thank You, Jesus! Amen.

EVENING

## When God Says No

*I consider that our present sufferings are not worth comparing with the glory that will be revealed in us.*

ROMANS 8:18 NIV

Father, why is it that people are sometimes not healed when they pray for healing? And why do moms and dads sometimes still get divorced even after their children have prayed for them to stay together? People die, and people get divorced. I don't understand, but I choose to praise You anyway. You want me to look beyond those things and see You. Because I know You love me, I will believe in You even when I don't understand. You see things clearly when I don't.

MORNING

## Fitness

*"Physical training is good, but training for godliness is much better, promising benefits in this life and in the life to come."*

1 Timothy 4:8 NLT

Father God, I love gymnastics. I'm really good on the balance beam, and I have strong skills for tumbling and the parallel bars. I train really hard. I'm getting better all the time, and I think I'll be ready to compete soon. God, You gave me skill and talent for gymnastics. Now I want to train just as hard to live a life that pleases You. Show me how to honor You with everything I do.

EVENING

## Even When They Don't Deserve It

*"The Lord is slow to anger, abounding in love and forgiving sin and rebellion. Yet he does not leave the guilty unpunished; he punishes the children for the sin of the parents to the third and fourth generation."*

Numbers 14:18 NIV

Lord, when people are mean and they hurt my feelings, I want to get back at them. I feel like being mean to them too. But then You remind me that it's not my job to punish them. You are the one in control, and You will see to it that they learn right from wrong. My role is to be like You, forgiving and loving others even when they don't deserve it. Amen.

MORNING

## Tell God About It

*If we confess our sins, he is faithful and just to forgive us our sins, and to cleanse us from all unrighteousness.*

1 JOHN 1:9 KJV

Dear God, when I sin, I don't like coming to You to pray. I feel guilty and I'm embarrassed. But You want me to come. You already know what I've done. If I tell You I'm sorry, I know You will forgive me. You promise to forgive me always, and You never fail to keep Your promises. I'm sorry for what I did. Please forgive me and help me to do better next time. Amen.

EVENING

## Happy to Know You!

*Yes, happy (blessed, fortunate, prosperous, to be envied) are the people whose God is the Lord!*

PSALM 144:15 AMPC

Just knowing You, Lord, is my greatest blessing. I feel safe with You. When I trust You, I know I'm in the right place. Nothing I could buy would fill my heart with happiness as much as You do. You lead me to accomplish good things. I have so much to celebrate because of You. You care about me. You love me, and that brings me joy. I'm happy to know You, Lord! Amen.

DAY 133

MORNING

## God Comforts Me

*"Blessed are those who mourn,*
*for they shall be comforted."*
MATTHEW 5:4 NKJV

Dear God, I'm sad. There are people I miss, and I wish we could be together. I'm sad because I have to stay inside instead of hanging out with my friends. Giving up activities I love makes me feel sad too. You are my safe place. When I get sad and teary, I come to You and tell You all about it. I feel better knowing You are here to comfort me. Amen.

EVENING

## Spotter

*"The God Who lives forever is your safe place.*
*His arms are always under you."*
DEUTERONOMY 33:27 NLV

In gymnastics, we have people called "spotters." They are ready with strong arms to catch us if we fall. You are like them, Lord. When I'm afraid, Your arms pull me close to You in a gentle hug. I can almost hear You say, "Don't worry. I'm here." If I fall into sin by doing something I know is wrong, Your strong arms will rescue me from that too. Thanks, Father God, for being my spotter. Amen.

# DAY 134

MORNING

## Jesus Forgives My Sins

*The Son of man hath power on earth to forgive sins.*

MARK 2:10 KJV

Jesus, no one has power to forgive sins like You do. You carried all my sins with You to the cross. I can't imagine Your pain as You hung there nailed to the cross, but You did it because You love me. Every sin I will ever do was forgiven on that day because of You. I will thank You by doing my best not to do what I know is wrong.

EVENING

## The Laws Given by Moses

*"Then you will do well, if you are careful to obey the Laws which the Lord gave to Israel by Moses. Be strong and have strength of heart. Do not be afraid or troubled."*

1 CHRONICLES 22:13 NLV

Dear God, the laws mentioned in tonight's Bible verse are the Ten Commandments, Your rules for living well found in Exodus 20:2–17. If I remember them and obey them, I will do well in life. Help me to think about them more often and do what they say. All Your rules are good. They make me strong and keep me from being afraid. Amen.

MORNING

# How I Use My Time

*Make the best use of your time. These are sinful days.*

EPHESIANS 5:16 NLV

Dear heavenly Father, I know You want me to make good use of my time. I don't always do that. I waste a lot of time messing around when I could be learning something. You have so many new opportunities waiting for me. Please lead me to them. Help me to become so interested in what You have to show me that I will want to spend all my time exploring and discovering. Amen.

EVENING

# My Teachers

*"Listen to me, O Judah and people of Jerusalem.*
*Trust in the Lord your God, and you will be made strong.*
*Trust in the men who speak for Him, and you will do well."*

2 CHRONICLES 20:20 NLV

Father God, You've put grown-ups in my life who trust You. They've known You longer than I have, and they know You better. These people are the teachers You have given me to help me grow stronger in my faith. Remind me to listen to them and learn. Keep me from being afraid to ask questions. Give them everything they need to teach me all about You. Amen.

DAY 136

MORNING

## My Behavior Honors God

*O God Who saves us, help us for the honor of Your name. Take us out of trouble and forgive our sins, for the honor of Your name.*

PSALM 79:9 NLV

Help me, God, to work on my behavior. My goal is to honor You with everything I say and do. I want to behave and talk in ways that obey Your rules. Please help me keep my heart clean of sin. I want my teachers and coaches, my friends' parents, and even strangers to tell my parents how well I behave. Then my parents can say, "That's because she honors God." Amen.

EVENING

## Eternal Life

*"I give them eternal life, and they shall never perish; no one will snatch them out of my hand."*

JOHN 10:28 NIV

Dear Father God, when the Bible says "eternal life," it means "living forever." You have existed forever, and so have Your Son, Jesus, and the Holy Spirit. I can't imagine what forever is like. Everything here on earth is about time. Things are born, and they die. But heaven, where You live, is forever. And when I get there one day, I will have eternal life there with You.

MORNING

## Decisions

*"But seek first the kingdom of God and His righteousness, and all these things shall be added to you."*

MATTHEW 6:33 NKJV

Father God, when I have a decision to make, I'm going to come to You first. I want to be sure that I'm going in the right direction. Before I decide, I will ask myself, *Will God approve of what I want to do?* Then I will talk with You about it. If I get in the habit of checking with You first, I know I'll make good decisions—decisions that please You. Amen.

EVENING

## A Little Faith

*"If you have faith as a mustard seed, you can say to this mulberry tree, 'Be pulled up by the roots and be planted in the sea,' and it would obey you."*

LUKE 17:6 NKJV

Dear Lord Jesus, amazing things happen when I have faith. I used to be afraid of the water. But I wanted to swim. I didn't have a lot of faith that I could learn, but I tried. With that little bit of faith, I took lessons. Now I'm an excellent swimmer, and I'm not afraid of the water anymore. Even a little faith is all it takes to do wonderful things.

# DAY 138

## MORNING

## It's Hard to Say No

*My sins are strong against me.*
*But You forgive our sins.*
PSALM 65:3 NLV

Dear Lord, when I want to do something I know is wrong, why is it so hard to say no? My mom trusted me to clean my room when I got home from school. I watched TV instead. When she got home, Mom was disappointed in me, and I was disappointed in myself too. You've already forgiven me, God, and Mom has too. But I really want to do better next time.

## EVENING

## God's Family

*"Whoever does God's will is my*
*brother and sister and mother."*
MARK 3:35 NIV

Dear God, Christians are everywhere! There are people living in every country of the world who believe in Jesus and trust Him as the one who saved them from sin. The Bible says they are my brothers and sisters in Christ. We are one big happy family of believers! Lead me to make friends with kids who know You. I want to build my own circle of Christian friends right here where I live. Amen.

MORNING

## God Is Good

*"Even when our sins speak against us, O Lord, do something for the good of Your name. For we have fallen away from You many times. We have sinned against You."*

JEREMIAH 14:7 NLV

Father, You are so good to me. Even when I'm at my worst, You continue to love and bless me. When it comes to sin, I keep stumbling and falling down. I don't mean to do things that displease You, but too often I don't stop myself. Still, You forgive me and bless me. Your goodness is all around me. Forgive me, Father, for my sins, and thank You for being my God. Amen.

EVENING

## Jesus' Love Is Perfect

*"No, the Father himself loves you because you have loved me and have believed that I came from God."*

JOHN 16:27 NIV

Jesus, I'm glad I'm part of Your family. My parents and my siblings are human, so they mess up sometimes. We get upset with each other and let each other down. But You are different. Your behavior and love for me are perfect. Instead of getting upset, You are patient with me. I can count on You all the time. You pour Your love on me because I've accepted You. Thank You for Your love. Amen.

## DAY 140

### MORNING

# Lost

*For the Son of man is come to seek*
*and to save that which was lost.*

LUKE 19:10 KJV

Dear Jesus, sometimes I feel lost. Everything seems upside down, and nothing makes me happy. When I feel that way, I feel apart from You. It's even hard to pray. But I know my lost feeling won't last long. You won't ever leave me; and if I leave You, I know You will find me. I will hear You in my heart, calling, "Here I am. Come to Me!" I'm coming, Jesus. Here I am. Amen.

### EVENING

# God Is on My Side

*The LORD is for me, so I will have no fear. What can mere people do to me? Yes, the LORD is for me; he will help me.*

PSALM 118:6–7 NLT

Why should I be afraid, God? You are on my side. You are more powerful than anything that gets in my way. I trust in Your power. When trouble comes, help me to keep my mind set on You. Remind me of Your words in the Bible. You always tell the truth. Your Word says, "Do not be afraid." I love and trust You, Lord. With You by my side, I'll be okay.

MORNING

## Getting Started

*The path of the lazy man is grown over with thorns, but the path of the faithful is a good road.*
PROVERBS 15:19 NLV

Dear Lord, the hardest part of any goal is getting started. I say I want to learn to play the piano. But I just mess around, hitting the keys and listening to the sounds they make. Learning to play means lessons and practice. That sounds like a lot of work. But if I want to learn, I can't be lazy. Remind me that I just need to start. Help me to take that first step. Amen.

EVENING

## Busy, Noisy World

*The LORD will give strength to His people; the LORD will bless His people with peace.*
PSALM 29:11 NKJV

Dear Father, my world gets really noisy sometimes. Too much is happening at once, and I need to get away. You are my quiet place. I like to go off by myself and just be with You for a while. When I tell You my troubles, You give me strength; but best of all, You fill me with Your peace. You make me ready to get back to my busy, noisy world.

DAY 142

MORNING

# Forgive Me, Lord

*To the Lord our God belong mercies and forgivenesses, though we have rebelled against him.*

DANIEL 9:9 KJV

Heavenly Father, sometimes I do what I want to do, when I want to do it. I don't think about what I know is right and good. I shut You out of my thoughts and go my own way. Even when I'm misbehaving, I know I'm doing wrong. But I do it anyway. I'm sorry, God. Please forgive me. Thank You for always forgiving me, even though I don't deserve it. Amen.

EVENING

# Look for the Lord

*Look for the Lord while He may be found. Call upon Him while He is near.*

ISAIAH 55:6 NLV

Lord, sometimes You seem far away. I think You feel far away from me so I will come looking for You. Without You, I feel lonely. I start making poor choices and behaving in ways that don't please You. When I recognize how much I need You, I pray a little longer and harder, and I read the Bible. When I look for You, I will find You. You didn't leave me—I left You.

MORNING

## Working for the Lord

*Whatever you do, work at it with all your heart, as working for the Lord, not for human masters.*

COLOSSIANS 3:23 NIV

Dear God, when there's hard work to do, I often don't want to do it. Mom says, "Get busy!" But that's the last thing I want to do. This morning's Bible verse is a good one because it reminds me that I'm working for You. With every good thing I do, no matter how hard, I'm pleasing You. Remembering that will help me to get busy and get the job done.

EVENING

## What Do You See?

*All of us, with no covering on our faces, show the shining-greatness of the Lord as in a mirror. All the time we are being changed to look like Him, with more and more of His shining-greatness. This change is from the Lord Who is the Spirit.*

2 CORINTHIANS 3:18 NLV

Lord, when You look at me, what do You see? You want me to be a reflection of You. It's not about how my body looks but about how the inside of my heart looks. Am I good, caring, and kind, like You? Am I forgiving? Is Jesus my example of how to behave, and do I behave like Him? Change me, Lord. Make me more like You. Amen.

DAY 144

MORNING

## Loving-Kindness

*"I will show loving-kindness to them and forgive their sins. I will remember their sins no more."*
HEBREWS 8:12 NLV

Father, I'm grateful for Your loving-kindness. You don't even remember the many times I've let You down. You truly forgive and forget. Teach me how to show loving-kindness to the people in my life and especially to those who haven't treated me well. I want to show them what unconditional love—love without expecting something in return—looks like. Thank You, Father, for loving me always without expectation. Amen.

EVENING

## I Will Tell Others About Jesus

*My Christian friends, you have obeyed me when I was with you. You have obeyed even more when I have been away. You must keep on working to show you have been saved from the punishment of sin. Be afraid that you may not please God.*
PHILIPPIANS 2:12 NLV

Jesus, I'm so thankful that You've saved me from my sins and made a way for me to get to heaven. I forget sometimes that there are people who don't know what You did for us. Some have never heard Your name. Remind me to tell my friends about You. Help me not to be afraid of their reaction. Your story is the most important of all—and You want me to tell it. Amen.

MORNING

# Difficult People

*Bear with each other and forgive one another if any of you has a grievance against someone.*

COLOSSIANS 3:13 NIV

Dear Lord, some people can be difficult to get along with. We're all different, and sometimes our personalities clash. But that's no reason for me not to be patient and kind. I know there will be people who say and do things that will irritate me today, but please help me not to let them get to me. Help me to remember that when I show understanding and forgiveness, I'm being like You. Amen.

EVENING

# God's Ways Are Perfect

*"As for God, His way is perfect. The Word of the Lord is proven true. He is a covering to all who go to Him to be safe."*

2 SAMUEL 22:31 NLV

Your way is always perfect, Lord. You will never send me in the wrong direction when I have a decision to make, when I'm confused, or when I wonder what my next step should be. Your Word guides me. The more I read the Bible, the more I will understand how to handle difficult situations. The Bible, along with talking with You, provides me with all I need. Lead me. Guide me in Your perfect way.

MORNING

# Forever Forgiving

*Who is a God like You, Who forgives sin and the wrong-doing of Your chosen people who are left? He does not stay angry forever because He is happy to show loving-kindness.*

MICAH 7:18 NLV

Heavenly Father, I keep messing up the same way over and over. I keep coming back asking for Your forgiveness for the same sin. I trust that You will forgive me every time, but I wonder if You do it willingly. The truth is—You do! You are always willing to forgive. You are happy to show me Your loving-kindness forever. How awesome is that! What would I do without You?

EVENING

# Think About It

*"This book of the Law must not leave your mouth. Think about it day and night, so you may be careful to do all that is written in it. Then all will go well with you. You will receive many good things."*

JOSHUA 1:8 NLV

Dear God, tonight's scripture verse reminds me of how important the Bible is. It's not enough that I read and memorize Bible verses. You want me to think about them day and night. If I don't understand what I read, You want me to ask questions. When I understand Your Word, I can be more careful to do what it says. Lead me, God. Guide me through the Bible. Amen.

MORNING

## Rejoice in Me!

*"The Lord your God in your midst, the Mighty One, will save; He will rejoice over you with gladness, He will quiet you with His love, He will rejoice over you with singing."*

Zephaniah 3:17 NKJV

Lord, I praise You for the little birds in our garden. They are so much fun to watch! You've thought of everything. You provide for all their needs, and You rejoice in it. Help me remember that, as much as I rejoice in watching the birds and listening to them sing, You rejoice in me even more. Thank You that I'm of more value to You than many birds. And thank You for them too. Amen.

EVENING

## Growing Daily

*As newborn babes, desire the sincere milk of the word, that ye may grow thereby.*

1 Peter 2:2 KJV

Father, I'm growing every day. It's been a long time since I was a baby. My body isn't the only thing growing. I'm growing in wisdom as I learn. Each day when I read the Bible, I'm growing stronger in my faith. Each time I memorize a Bible verse, I'm building my strength against trouble. Like a baby needs milk, I need the Word of God. The Bible is necessary for me to grow. Amen.

DAY 148

MORNING

## The Reset Button

*"I, even I, am the One Who takes away your sins because of Who I am. And I will not remember your sins."*

ISAIAH 43:25 NLV

Dear God, You are so wonderful. I needed the computer for my homework last night, but I couldn't get on the internet. I knew to hit the RESET button on the router, and that worked! Then I thought of You. Whenever I sin and do something to displease You, You hit the RESET button! You take away my sin and let me start over again. I appreciate You, God, and I thank You. Amen.

EVENING

## I'll Be Happy Again

*"You are sad now. I will see you again and then your hearts will be full of joy. No one can take your joy from you."*

JOHN 16:22 NLV

Jesus, when I feel sad, I run to You because You always make me feel better. Just knowing You are there waiting for me makes me happy. I can tell You anything. I know You are already working out my problems. You comfort me. As soon as I pray, I feel my sadness going away. You are my best friend, and You help me let go of my troubles so I can be happy again.

MORNING

## Far, Far Away

*As far as the east is from the west, so far hath he removed our transgressions from us.*

PSALM 103:12 KJV

Father, I get upset with myself sometimes. I want to do better, but then I just. . .don't. You know that one sinful thing that keeps getting me. I fall for it every time. I know it's wrong, but I do it anyway. I worry You might be upset with me, but You're not. When I come to You and say I'm sorry, You remove that sin from me as far as the east is from the west.

EVENING

## Perfectly Trustworthy

*Thou wilt keep him in perfect peace, whose mind is stayed on thee: because he trusteth in thee.*

ISAIAH 26:3 KJV

Dear Father God, I need to trust You more. Tonight's Bible verse says I will have peace if I keep my mind set on You. I worry about stuff. I don't usually feel peaceful inside. But if I can build trust in You and Your promises, I know You'll replace my worry with Your peace. You are perfectly trustworthy; so please, God, help me to trust You more. Amen.

DAY 150

MORNING

## Starry, Starry Night

*He knows the number of the stars. He gives names to all of them. Great is our Lord, and great in power. His understanding has no end.*

PSALM 147:4–5 NLV

Heavenly Father, I love going outside on a warm night and looking at the stars. How many are there? You know. You've counted them all, and You've given them names. You know each star just like You know every person on earth. There's nothing You don't know. My mind imagines You as something I can understand, but You are so much more. Your power is beyond anything human. Who is like You? No one.

EVENING

## Untroubled Heart

*"Peace I leave with you; my peace I give you. I do not give to you as the world gives. Do not let your hearts be troubled and do not be afraid."*

JOHN 14:27 NIV

Dear God, I'm troubled about something, and the trouble seems really big. There are so many parts to it, and they're so tangled up that I can't make sense of it all. I have no idea what to do about it. But You know how to untangle the problem and heal my heart. So I give it to You, God. Here is my problem. Untangle it, heal my heart, and give me peace. Amen.

MORNING

## Behind God's Back

*"You have kept my soul from the grave that destroys. You have put all my sins behind Your back."*

ISAIAH 38:17 NLV

Dear Father, I can't see what is behind me. It's like it doesn't even exist. I have to imagine that if You put something behind Your back, it doesn't really exist anymore. You don't want to look at it, think about it, or even be bothered by it. That is what You have done about my past sins. You've put them behind You. They no longer matter to You. Remind me of that, God. Amen.

EVENING

## A Not-So-Joyful Day

*Light shines on the righteous and joy on the upright in heart. Rejoice in the LORD, you who are righteous, and praise his holy name.*

PSALM 97:11–12 NIV

I may not feel joyful right now, Lord, but just because today doesn't feel wonderful doesn't mean You have forgotten me. You still guide me and lead me. Your light and Your love will shine upon me and make me feel happy again. Thank You for being there, willing to help me, on good days and bad. I praise You for Your faithfulness to me, Lord, no matter what I experience. Amen.

## MORNING

# Praise!

*The poor will eat and be satisfied; those who seek the LORD will praise him—may your hearts live forever!*

PSALM 22:26 NIV

Dear heavenly Father, whenever I call on You, whenever I need You, You are there. If You seem far away, it's because I have left You and not because You left me. When I look for You, I will find You. You will never hide from me. You provide everything I need, and each day I'm satisfied. I praise You for always being with me, for loving me, and just for being my God. Amen.

## EVENING

# When Someone Dies

*"When this that can be destroyed has been changed into that which cannot be destroyed. . .then it will happen as the Holy Writings said it would happen. They said, "Death has no more power over life."*

1 CORINTHIANS 15:54 NLV

Dear God, when someone we know dies, it's like a big hole opens inside our hearts and all our tears can't fill it. Remembering that the one who died is with You helps. Since there is no sadness in heaven, when people die, they aren't sad they aren't on earth anymore. Death has no power over them. Tonight, Lord, please comfort those who have lost loved ones. Dry their tears and bring them peace.

MORNING

## Every Animal Belongs to Him

*"For every animal of the forest is mine,*
*and the cattle on a thousand hills."*
Psalm 50:10 NIV

Father God, I wonder how many different kinds of animals You have created. I'm sure some of the animals You made in the beginning don't exist anymore. Your animals have fur, feathers, or scales. They live in forests, under water, in deserts, and on mountains. You know each animal and call them by name. All the animals on earth belong to You, God. You made them, and they are Yours.

EVENING

## Taught by the Master

*And all thy children shall be taught of the Lord;*
*and great shall be the peace of thy children.*
Isaiah 54:13 KJV

I have lots of good teachers, God, but there is no teacher greater than You. When I learn from You, I can discover all I need to know about the world and the people around me. I know I will learn my lessons well because I'm being taught by the Master. Help me to be a good student, Father. You have so much to teach me, and I want to learn. Amen.

MORNING

## The Depths of the Sea

*He will have compassion upon us; he will subdue our iniquities; and thou wilt cast all their sins into the depths of the sea.*

MICAH 7:19 KJV

Father, I learned that, on average, oceans are about two miles deep. The deeper a person travels to the ocean floor, the darker it gets. Whatever sinks to the bottom lies silently there, never to be seen again. This morning's Bible verse says You will throw my sins to the bottom of the darkest, deepest ocean—never to be thought of again. Thank You for that, God. My sins are forgotten and forever gone!

EVENING

## Strength and Peace

*The LORD will give strength unto his people; the LORD will bless his people with peace.*

PSALM 29:11 KJV

Dear God, Your power could move mountains, drain oceans, or snatch the moon and sun from the sky. Still, You are so calm with me. You are like a dad playing with a baby. Your arms are powerful and strong, but Your hands are soft and kind. I feel at peace knowing You are strong enough to stop anything that tries to hurt me, yet gentle enough to hold me close and love me.

MORNING

## New Clothes

*The angel said to those who were standing in front of him, "Take off his dirty clothes." And he said to him, "See, I have taken your sin away from you, and will dress you in beautiful clothes."*
ZECHARIAH 3:4 NLV

Dear Lord, this morning's verse reminds me of a field trip when I was little. We went to a farm, and I fell in the mud. My clothes were covered with the goo. So was my hair! Getting clean and putting on fresh clothes felt so good. Sin is like that. It makes me feel dirty. When You forgive me, it's like putting on fresh, new clothes. Thank You, Lord! Amen.

EVENING

## God, the Great Creator

*For by him were all things created, that are in heaven, and that are in earth, visible and invisible, whether they be thrones, or dominions, or principalities, or powers: all things were created by him, and for him.*
COLOSSIANS 1:16 KJV

God, in the beginning, You spoke the world into existence. You said words like "Let there be light" (Genesis 1:3) and "Let the earth bring into being living things after their kind: Cattle and things that move upon the ground, and wild animals of the earth after their kind" (Genesis 1:24 NLV). Whatever You said—it happened! You haven't changed. Even today when You, the great Creator, speak, whatever You say happens. How great and mighty You are!

## DAY 156

### MORNING

# I Spy

*I will set no sinful thing in front of my eyes.*

PSALM 101:3 NLV

Heavenly Father, sin comes at us through all our senses. On television and in videos, we see people doing things that don't please You. And our watching those shows doesn't please You either. Things we choose to look at can lead us away from You. Please help me to be careful about what I watch. Guide me instead toward seeing all the beautiful things You've put into the world for me to enjoy. Amen.

### EVENING

# A Shining Light

*In that way, you can prove yourselves to be without blame. You are God's children and no one can talk against you, even in a sin-loving and sin-sick world. You are to shine as lights among the sinful people of this world.*

PHILIPPIANS 2:15 NLV

Light makes me feel good, Father. On dark, rainy days, I don't feel like doing much at all. But when the sun shines brightly, I'm filled with energy and ready to go. You say we are to shine like lights among sinful people. That's what I want to do. I want my friends and neighbors—and even people I don't know—to see You in me. Let me be a light for You, Father. Amen.

MORNING

## Sprinkled!

*Then will I sprinkle clean water upon you, and ye shall be clean: from all your filthiness, and from all your idols, will I cleanse you.*

EZEKIEL 36:25 KJV

Dear God, nothing feels better on a hot summer day than running through a sprinkler. That cold water raining down on me when I run barefoot in the grass is so refreshing. Instead of feeling hot and sweaty, I feel clean! It reminds me, Lord, of how good it feels when You wash me clean of my sins. Whatever sinful thing I do, I know I can count on Your forgiveness. Thank You!

EVENING

## The Joy of the Lord Is My Strength

*The joy of the LORD is your strength.*

NEHEMIAH 8:10 KJV

God, I've been so busy. I've been trying hard to get everything done, and I'm tired. There have been moments when I thought I couldn't take another step. The truth is that I can't move forward without You. But You are with me! You want to take the pressure off me and give me strength. Knowing that I can count on You gives me joy. Make me strong, Lord. Let's get this done together.

DAY 158

MORNING

## God's Great Love

*For great is his love toward us, and the faithfulness of the LORD endures forever. Praise the LORD.*

PSALM 117:2 NIV

I know You love me, Lord, but I can't imagine how much. Your love is too great for me to understand. It isn't an ordinary kind of love. You've loved me forever, and Your love for me will never end. Each day, as I learn more about You, my love for You grows. I have so much to praise You for! Everything I have and every good thing I accomplish is because You love me.

EVENING

## Surprises

*For the LORD thy God bringeth thee into a good land, a land of brooks of water, of fountains and depths that spring out of valleys and hills.*

DEUTERONOMY 8:7 KJV

Dear Lord, I praise You for the surprising ways You love me. Thank You for the way rain droplets cover a branch like diamonds. Thank You for the pictures You paint with sunrises and sunsets. Thank You for the colorful flowers that pop up in spring, even when there is some snow left on the ground. Thank You for how You delight in surprising me with the beauty of Your world. Amen.

MORNING

## I Forgive You

*And when ye stand praying, forgive, if ye have ought against any: that your Father also which is in heaven may forgive you your trespasses.*

MARK 11:25 KJV

Dear Lord, when I pray, I remember to thank You for my blessings, I tell You what's on my mind, and I usually ask You for something. I forget, though, to ask You to help me forgive those who were mean to me or hurt my feelings. You say that my forgiving others ties to You forgiving me. I need to remember to put forgiveness first in my prayers. Thank You for reminding me. Amen.

EVENING

## In the Right Direction

*He guides the humble in what is right and teaches them his way.*

PSALM 25:9 NIV

Dear Father God, sometimes I think I have all the answers. When I do things my way, they don't always turn out. But when I stop and listen to Your words in my heart—when I follow Your way—I know You will guide me in the right direction. Teach me what is right, Father. Show me which way I should go. I'm listening. Amen.

## DAY 160

### MORNING

# Let's Go!

*In the same way, faith by itself, if it is not accompanied by action, is dead.*

JAMES 2:17 NIV

God, there are things I want to do—*big* things, things I wonder if I'm good enough to accomplish. I have faith that You will help me all along the way. My problem is I talk about doing those things, but I never take that first step. Like today's Bible verse says, faith not accompanied by action is dead. Help me to take the first step. I'm ready to act. Let's go! Amen.

### EVENING

# Trust

*"Even though He would kill me, yet I will trust in Him."*

JOB 13:15 NLV

Father, I say I trust You, but I wonder how far my trust goes. If You seemed very far away, if You didn't answer my requests the way I expected, would I still trust You? If trouble followed me everywhere and I didn't feel You helping me, would I trust You then? You want me to trust You no matter what! Please help me. Build up my trust until nothing can get between me and You.

MORNING

# Let Your Light Shine!

*"Let your light so shine before men, that they may see your good works and glorify your Father in heaven."*

MATTHEW 5:16 NKJV

Dear Jesus, I want to tell others about You. I want everyone to be close to You, the way I am. But sometimes it's hard. Some of my friends aren't Christians, and when I talk about You, they make fun of me. I try not to let it get to me. Instead, I let my light shine. That means I show them through my behavior what it's like to know and follow You. Amen.

EVENING

# They're Watching Me

*When you are around people who do not know God, be careful how you act. Even if they talk against you as wrong-doers, in the end they will give thanks to God for your good works when Christ comes again.*

1 PETER 2:12 NLV

Dear God, I want my behavior always to honor You. Remind me that people who don't know You are watching me, wondering if I'll behave according to what the Bible teaches. If I mess up with my talk or actions, I send the message that I'm not really following You. Help me to behave in ways that are good and pleasing to You. Then lead nonbelievers to want to follow You too.

## DAY 162

MORNING

# Count to Ten

*A man's understanding makes him slow to anger.*
*It is to his honor to forgive and forget a wrong done to him.*
PROVERBS 19:11 NLV

Father, sometimes I feel really angry. I mean, I get so mad that I want to stomp my feet and yell. But then I remember it honors You to forgive and forget when someone or something makes me angry. So I try to calm down and slowly count to ten, and then I begin to feel that anger lift. I pray too, asking You to help me, and pretty soon the anger is gone.

EVENING

# I Want More

*There is one who pretends to be rich, but has nothing.*
*Another pretends to be poor, but has many riches.*
PROVERBS 13:7 NLV

Lord, sometimes I want more. I think about buying cool shoes and clothes that cost a lot of money. I imagine my family taking vacations to wonderful places and not having to worry about how much it costs. But then I remember I don't need to be rich and have lots of money. I'm rich because I have You. You are all I want and need, and everything I have is a blessing. Amen.

MORNING

## Up, Up, and Away!

*He brought me up out of the hole of danger, out of the mud and clay. He set my feet on a rock, making my feet sure. He put a new song in my mouth, a song of praise to our God. Many will see and fear and will put their trust in the Lord.*

Psalm 40:2–3 NLV

Dear Father, yesterday I was troubled about that thing I had to do, but You brought me through it just fine! You lifted me up out of my fear and gave me courage. I felt You with me through it all, and we did it together. You always lift me up when I'm worried or afraid. We walk troubled paths side by side. Oh, how I praise You, Lord! Thank You. Amen.

EVENING

## Planting Seeds

*Remember, the man who plants only a few seeds will not have much grain to gather. The man who plants many seeds will have much grain to gather.*

2 Corinthians 9:6 NLV

Heavenly Father, tonight's Bible verse reminds me that how I behave is like planting seeds. Seeds of caring, kindness, forgiveness, and love will grow into something good and beautiful. But if I plant bad seeds like selfishness, anger, lying, and disrespect, those will grow to be ugly, like weeds. Father, help me to always honor You with my behavior. I want all the seeds I plant to be good. Amen.

MORNING

# Do Good to Them

*Do good to them that hate you, and pray for them which despitefully use you, and persecute you.*

MATTHEW 5:44 KJV

Father, bless those who have hurt me. Bless those who have hurt people I love. It's hard to love someone who is mean and angry, but that's what You want me to do. I ask You to show me how to be kind and caring, even to those who aren't. Help me to pray for them; and God, please help them to turn away from being hurtful and act in ways that please You.

EVENING

# Courage

*"Be strong and very courageous. Be careful to obey all the law my servant Moses gave you; do not turn from it to the right or to the left, that you may be successful wherever you go."*

JOSHUA 1:7 NIV

Dear Father God, when I trust in Your promises in the Bible, I can't go wrong. It's only when I turn away from You that I get into trouble. It takes courage to follow Your ways instead of following my friends. But I trust that when they try to lead me the wrong way, You will give me the strength to say no. Thank You for always guiding me down the right path. Amen.

MORNING

# A Little (a Lot of!) Respect

*"Respect and give thanks for those who try to bring bad to you. Pray for those who make it very hard for you."*

LUKE 6:28 NLV

Dear Jesus, how did You do it? How were You able to respect and give thanks for those who made it very hard for You? This morning's Bible verse reminds me to try to behave more like You. Teach me to be respectful to those who don't respect me. Give me the right words to pray for those who make it hard for me. Make me more like You. Amen.

EVENING

# Be Content

*Keep your lives free from the love of money.*
*Be happy with what you have. God has said,*
*"I will never leave you or let you be alone."*

HEBREWS 13:5 NLV

Dear God, there's a girl in my class who is kind of stuck-up. She has lots of nice things, and she talks about them all the time. She wears designer clothes. Her parents bought her a phone and other cool things. But she doesn't have many friends. I'm content with what I have, God. And even if I were like her, without many friends, I know You would never let me be alone. Amen.

MORNING

## A Holy Fire

*For our God is a fire that destroys everything.*

HEBREWS 12:29 NLV

Lord, You have power over everything on earth, in the sky, and in heaven. There's nothing You can't do. You don't put up with evil. Like a holy fire, You rush in and turn it to dust. When trouble comes my way, I don't need to worry because You are on my side. Before I even call out, You come and help me, destroying anything that gets in my way. Thank You, God! Amen.

EVENING

## In Your Footsteps

*The Spirit of God, who raised Jesus from the dead, lives in you.*

ROMANS 8:11 NLT

Jesus, thank You for providing a way for me to belong to Your Father's family. When You created me, You planned for me to love and follow You. I will do my best to follow in Your footsteps. I want to be like You. I want to behave toward others the way You did. I'm grateful to be part of Your family. Jesus, ours is the greatest family—in heaven and on earth! Amen.

MORNING

## Inside My Heart

*The spirit of a man is the lamp of the LORD,*
*searching all the inner depths of his heart.*
PROVERBS 20:27 NKJV

Lord, what do You see when You search my spirit and look into my heart? I hope You'll see only good things. I try to honor You with my actions and words. I tell others about how great You are, hoping they will decide to follow You. You've already forgiven my sins—so when You look inside my heart, I hope You'll find it nice and clean, a good place for You to live. Amen.

EVENING

## Take It Back

*If we confess our sins, He is faithful and just to forgive us*
*our sins and to cleanse us from all unrighteousness.*
1 JOHN 1:9 NKJV

Lord, I wish I could start today over. I wish I could take back my attitude and words. I messed up badly. Sometimes it's difficult for me to understand why You still love me. Please forgive me. Help me to remember the next time I feel frustrated and impatient to turn to You before I do or say something I'll be sorry for. Thank You for forgiving me, Father. Now please help me to forgive myself.

# DAY 168

## MORNING

# I'm Praying for Him

*When someone does something bad to you, do not do the same thing to him. When someone talks about you, do not talk about him. Instead, pray that good will come to him. You were called to do this so you might receive good things from God.*

1 PETER 3:9 NLV

Dear God, I'm praying for him. You know who. He's so mean and disrespectful to me. But every day I pray that good will come to him. I don't see him changing, but I trust that You are working on him, so I'll continue to pray. I know it pleases You when I pray for him, and I believe You will bless me for it—that's Your promise in this morning's Bible verse. Amen.

## EVENING

# Jesus Lives in Me

*I have been crucified with Christ and I no longer live, but Christ lives in me. The life I now live in the body, I live by faith in the Son of God, who loved me and gave himself for me.*

GALATIANS 2:20 NIV

Jesus, when I accepted You as Lord and Savior, You came to live inside my heart. Nothing has been the same since. You gave Your life for me! If You were willing to do that, I have faith that You would do anything for me. I trust You to love and care for me, not just now but forever. Thank You, Jesus, for saving me from sin and wanting to live in my heart. Amen.

MORNING

## Patience and Practice

*We speak kind words to those who speak against us. When people hurt us, we say nothing.*

1 CORINTHIANS 4:12 NLV

Dear Lord, I'm trying. You say I should speak kind words to those who are unkind to me; and if someone hurts me, I should say nothing. I'm sure You don't mean I shouldn't tell a grown-up if someone hurts me. But not talking back to those who hurt my feelings takes a lot of patience and practice. Please help with that, Lord. Help my words to always be a reflection of You. Amen.

EVENING

## Good News

*But you are a chosen group of people. You are the King's religious leaders. You are a holy nation. You belong to God. He has done this for you so you can tell others how God has called you out of darkness into His great light.*

1 PETER 2:9 NLV

Father, You created me; You made me Your child; and You have chosen me to tell the good news to others. The good news is that Jesus died for our sins and He is our way to heaven. Teach me how to share it with others. Show me who needs to hear it. I want everyone I know, and strangers too, to hear the story of Jesus. I pray they will choose to follow Him. Amen.

MORNING

# John 3:16

*"For God so loved the world that He gave His only begotten Son, that whoever believes in Him should not perish but have everlasting life."*

JOHN 3:16 NKJV

Dear God, John 3:16 was the first Bible verse I memorized. In just a few words, it tells the story of Jesus. Because You love us, You sent Your Son to save us from sin. And all of us who believe He died for our sins have the promise of living forever in heaven. If I get stuck finding the words to tell others about Your Son, I can always remember John 3:16. Amen.

EVENING

# Back on Track

*I will instruct you and teach you in the way you should go; I will guide you with My eye.*

PSALM 32:8 NKJV

Heavenly Father, a GPS is supposed to work all the time, but the one in our car failed while we were on vacation. It kept saying, "Recalculating," and sending us in circles. Tonight's Bible verse reminds me that You will never allow me to get lost. You are watching me all the time, and I trust You to use Your eyes to guide me back to the right path. Amen.

MORNING

## Keep Me Safe

*Keep me safe as You would Your own eye.*
*Hide me in the shadow of Your wings.*
PSALM 17:8 NLV

Dear God, some of Your blessings I can see; others go unseen. I'm sure that many times You've kept me and my family from harm and we didn't even know it. You put us in the right places at the right times to keep us out of danger. I'm grateful that You are always watching and take such good care of us. Thank You, God, for Your blessings, and thank You for keeping us safe.

EVENING

## Brand New!

*Anyone who belongs to Christ has become a new person. The old life is gone; a new life has begun!*
2 CORINTHIANS 5:17 NLT

Dear Jesus, when someone accepts You as their Lord and Savior, You give them a brand-new life. The Bible says their old life is gone and a new life has begun. That's because You've taken away all their sins—the bad things they've done in the past. And You have already forgiven any bad things they will do in the future. All they have to do is ask. I think that's so cool! Amen.

DAY 172

MORNING

# Kill It with Kindness

*"If the one who hates you is hungry, feed him. If he is thirsty, give him water. If you do that, you will be making him more ashamed of himself."*

ROMANS 12:20 NLV

Dear Father God, when a girl in my class was being mean to me, my grandma told me, "Kill it with kindness." Of course, she didn't *really* mean to kill anything. She was just reminding me to do what the Bible says in Romans 12:20. If I react to meanness with kindness, it pleases You. And it might even make the mean person feel a little ashamed of herself too. Amen.

EVENING

# In God's Image

*"Live out your God-created identity. Live generously and graciously toward others, the way God lives toward you."*

MATTHEW 5:48 MSG

Dear God, You created me in Your image. That means You created me to have a spirit like Yours. You made me to be like You: generous, kind, gentle, patient, forgiving, slow to anger, and so much more! It's my job to live in ways that show others Your Spirit. I'll make a list, God, of all the good things You are and then do my best to be like You. Amen.

MORNING

## Let God Take Care of It

*Do not say, "I will punish wrong-doing." Wait on the Lord, and He will take care of it.*

PROVERBS 20:22 NLV

Dear Lord, I'm not very good at waiting patiently. And I'm also not very good at not fighting back. When people say or do mean things to me, my first instinct is to do the same to them. But that's not what You want. Help me, please, to remember to give my problem to You and wait patiently, trusting that You will take care of it. Thank You, Lord. Amen.

EVENING

## A Compassionate Heart

*Be kind and compassionate to one another, forgiving each other, just as in Christ God forgave you.*

EPHESIANS 4:32 NIV

Dear heavenly Father, Your compassion—Your caring and loving-kindness—for us is so great it can't be measured. Your constant love for us is huge. When You see someone in need, You provide for them. You comfort those who are sad. Father, please create in me a heart filled with compassion like Yours. Help me never to be so busy that I overlook helping people who are in need. Amen.

## DAY 174

### MORNING

# Siblings

*Whoever claims to love God yet hates a brother or sister is a liar. For whoever does not love their brother and sister, whom they have seen, cannot love God, whom they have not seen.*

1 John 4:20 NIV

Dear God, thank You for my siblings. I know that whenever I'm in trouble, I can always count on them. Sometimes we argue a lot, but we always make up. We know how much we love one another, and silly little fights aren't going to get in the way. I pray we'll always be there for each other even when we're all grown up. Bless my sisters and brothers today. Amen.

### EVENING

# A True Friend

*"Is this your kindness to your friend? Why did you not go with your friend?"*

2 Samuel 16:17 NLV

Dear Jesus, I want to be a true friend. Help me to be trustworthy, reliable, and forgiving. Remind me to put my friends' needs ahead of my own. Lead me to encourage my friends and to stand up for them if others put them down. I want to be the kind of friend who is loving and always ready to help. Make me into a better friend, Jesus—a true friend like You. Amen.

MORNING

## I Am Willing

*Jesus reached out his hand and touched the man. "I am willing," he said. "Be clean!" Immediately he was cleansed of his leprosy.*

MATTHEW 8:3 NIV

Jesus, You are always willing to help. When You lived on earth—even when You were around people with a disease that was contagious—You stepped right up to help. You touched a man with a skin disease and healed him. Jesus, guide me to be a ready helper like You. If I see someone in need and I can help, don't let anything stop me. I am willing!

EVENING

## Perfect Counselor

*"He will not speak on His own authority, but whatever He hears He will speak; and He will tell you things to come."*

JOHN 16:13 NKJV

God, when I have a problem, I sometimes ask for advice, and I still end up confused. Maybe that's because I didn't go to You first. You are the perfect counselor. You know the answers to my questions, and You will never lead me the wrong way. No one can guide me as You can. Thank You for Your perfect guidance. Help me to seek You first and to obey Your voice in my heart. Amen.

MORNING

## Fighting Back

*"But I tell you, do not fight with the man who wants to fight. Whoever hits you on the right side of the face, turn so he can hit the other side also."*

MATTHEW 5:39 NLV

Dear Jesus, You often taught using examples. In this morning's verse, I don't think You really meant it's okay for someone to hit me and especially to hit me more than once. I think You meant I should walk away from fights instead of fighting back. Teach me, Jesus, what You meant when You said this. I sometimes have trouble understanding. Give me a heart that wants to follow Your example. Amen.

EVENING

## The Words of My Mouth

*May the words of my mouth and the meditation of my heart be pleasing to you, O LORD, my rock and my redeemer.*

PSALM 19:14 NLT

Dear God, words have power. Words can be kind and loving, or they can be cold and hurtful. Often, before I open my mouth and speak, I don't think about whether my words will be pleasing to You. I say what's on my mind and then regret it. Help me to be better at controlling what I say. I want the words of my mouth to honor You. Thank You, Father. Amen.

MORNING

## Be a Messenger

*Do not let anyone pay back for the bad he received. But look for ways to do good to each other and to all people.*

1 THESSALONIANS 5:15 NLV

Father, the words in the Bible are wise. They've taught me many things. I think You want me to pass Your words and lessons on to others. If I see friends planning to get even for something bad that happened to them, I can tell them that's not what You want. You want us to always do good to each other. Help me to be Your messenger. Give me the right words to say.

EVENING

## Completely and Forever

*People with their minds set on you, you keep completely whole, steady on their feet, because they keep at it and don't quit.*

ISAIAH 26:3 MSG

Lord God, I tell my troubles to You. I share my problems, and I give them to You to work out. But it doesn't take long before I take those troubles and problems back, trying to work them out on my own. I don't know why I do that. I trust You. I know You'll work everything out. Forgive me for making my problems even bigger by not giving them to You completely and forever.

MORNING

## The Promise Keeper

*For no matter how many promises God has made, they are "Yes" in Christ.*

2 CORINTHIANS 1:20 NIV

Dear Father, how many times have I promised my parents I would do something and I didn't? How many times have I promised my baby sister I'd read to her or play dolls and I didn't? How many times did I promise to call my grandparents and I didn't? Forgive me for breaking my promises. You always keep Your promises—every one! Teach me what it means to be that kind of promise keeper. Amen.

EVENING

## God, Be My Teacher

*My son, pay attention to what I say; turn your ear to my words. Do not let them out of your sight, keep them within your heart; for they are life to those who find them and health to one's whole body.*

PROVERBS 4:20–22 NIV

God, I invite You to be my teacher, to lead and guide me to learn Your ways. Show me how to listen for Your voice in my heart. Help me when I read the Bible to understand its words. Remind me to think about You all day long and to keep my eyes open to Your presence. I'll go where You want me to go today. Help me to focus my energy on Your instructions.

MORNING

## My Plans, God's Purpose

*People can make all kinds of plans,*
*but only the LORD's plan will happen.*
PROVERBS 19:21 NCV

Heavenly Father, plans change. When they do, I think it's You reminding me that You have another purpose for my day. Instead of being disappointed when my plans don't work out, I will remember to seek You and talk with You in prayer. Help me to step aside if I am getting in Your way. I want Your plans to come before mine because You always know the way I should go. Amen.

EVENING

## Love Even When It's Hard

*Love takes everything that comes without*
*giving up. Love believes all things. Love hopes*
*for all things. Love keeps on in all things.*
1 CORINTHIANS 13:7 NLV

Give me a loving heart, God. When people hurt my feelings, help me look for the best in them. Remind me that love is an everyday action and not just when I feel like it. Help me to love others even when loving them is hard. Help me to show love not only in actions but also in words. When I love people, God, it's like You loving them through me. Amen.

# DAY 180

## MORNING

# Angels

*For He will give His angels [especial] charge over you to accompany and defend and preserve you in all your ways [of obedience and service].*

PSALM 91:11 AMPC

Dear Lord, the Bible says we are accompanied by Your angels. They go with us and protect us. They keep evil away. Whenever I'm going somewhere I haven't been before and I'm a little afraid or uncertain, I will remember that Your angels will go with me. I'll be aware of them, even though I can't see them. Thank You, God, for the invisible angels that surround me all the time. Amen.

## EVENING

# I Didn't Deserve It

*But if you bear patiently with suffering [which results] when you do right and that is undeserved, it is acceptable and pleasing to God.*

1 PETER 2:20 AMPC

Father, I didn't deserve that. I thought she was my friend, but then she did something that really hurt my feelings. I can't stop thinking about it, and I'm very sad. You saw what happened, and You know I did everything right. The Bible says that it's pleasing to You when I do what's right. Father, I'm waiting patiently for You to work things out. Please comfort me. Help me to feel better. Amen.

MORNING

# Stay Alert!

*Stay alert! Watch out for your great enemy, the devil. He prowls around like a roaring lion, looking for someone to devour.*

1 PETER 5:8 NLT

Dear Father God, I was thinking this morning about the story of Adam and Eve and how the sneaky serpent, the devil, tricked Eve into doing what You said was forbidden. Sin can be tricky. If I'm not careful, I know that I can be tricked into doing things that don't please You. Help me to stay alert. If I get close to doing what's wrong, remind me to say no. Amen.

EVENING

# Inside, Outside

*Pleasing ways lie and beauty comes to nothing, but a woman who fears the Lord will be praised.*

PROVERBS 31:30 NLV

Dear Jesus, sometimes I see women who are beautiful on the outside, but their behavior tells me they aren't as beautiful on the inside. What's inside is what matters to You. When I grow up, I want to be the kind of woman who people look at and say, "She follows Jesus!" I won't care if they think I'm not beautiful on the outside. When they see me, I want them to see You. Amen.

## DAY 182

### MORNING

# Quarrels

*Try to understand other people. Forgive each other. If you have something against someone, forgive him. That is the way the Lord forgave you.*

COLOSSIANS 3:13 NLV

Dear Jesus, my brother and I quarrel about silly, little things. He gets on my nerves sometimes. I don't understand why, but he just irritates me. Will You help me, please, to understand him better? I don't want to argue or fight with him. Right here and now, I forgive him for all the times he's picked on me. Help us to get along better. He's my brother, and I love him.

### EVENING

# I'm Responsible for Myself

*Each of you must take responsibility for doing the creative best you can with your own life.*

GALATIANS 6:5 MSG

You give me rules to live by, God, but it's my responsibility to follow them. I'm in charge of my behavior, and it's up to me to do the very best I can with my life. When I promise myself to do better, help me to keep my promise. Lead me to become the person You created me to be. I have a long life ahead of myself, and I want to live it well.

MORNING

## All Praise Him!

*Then I heard every living thing in heaven and on the earth and under the earth and in the sea and all that are in them. They were saying, "Thanks and honor and shining-greatness and all power are to the One Who sits on the throne and to the Lamb forever."*

REVELATION 5:13 NLV

Dear God, I wonder what it would sound like if every human and everything You created on earth and in heaven all praised You at the same time. I think it would be very loud, but in a good way. I imagine it would be the most beautiful music ever heard in heaven and on earth. I praise You, God! I praise You, Jesus! Amen.

EVENING

## Seeking Peace

*Consider the blameless, observe the upright;*
*a future awaits those who seek peace.*

PSALM 37:37 NIV

Heavenly Father, I want peace. Not just peace for myself but for everyone. The television news is usually about bad stuff happening. People are disagreeing about a lot of stuff. They don't get along. Peace comes when we put You first and do what Jesus said: "Love one another." God, please help me to bring some peace to the world by following Your commands and doing my best to get along with everyone.

DAY 184

MORNING

## Tenderhearted

*Be ye kind one to another, tenderhearted, forgiving one another, even as God for Christ's sake hath forgiven you.*

EPHESIANS 4:32 KJV

God, a tender heart is caring and gentle. Your heart is tender toward me. You show how much You care by gently forgiving me for my sins instead of getting angry and punishing me. You are quick to help me and comfort me when I need it. I want to be tenderhearted toward others. Fill me with Your kindness, gentleness, and caring ways. Help me to forgive others just as You forgive me.

EVENING

## No Shortcuts

*For we cannot oppose the truth,*
*but must always stand for the truth.*

2 CORINTHIANS 13:8 NLT

Lord, sometimes doing what's right is really hard. When my friend wants to do something You won't approve of, I should say no and tell her why I think it's wrong. Instead, I take a shortcut. I make an excuse and walk away or, worse, go along with her. I want to stand up for what I know is right. Help me not to be afraid to say, "This is wrong because. . ." Amen.

MORNING

## My Mom

*"As one whom his mother comforts,*
*so I will comfort you."*
ISAIAH 66:13 NASB

Dear God, You gave me the most awesome mom. No one on earth loves me the way she does. She works hard for our family. She makes our house a safe and happy place. She makes the best meals, and she puts little notes in my backpack to remind me all day long that she loves me. Best of all, when I'm sick or sad, she comforts me. Thank You, God, for my amazing mom.

EVENING

## I Will Be a Good Example

*You yourself must be an example to them by doing good works of every kind. Let everything you do reflect the integrity and seriousness of your teaching.*
TITUS 2:7 NLT

Father, You've taught me about how You want me to live. Now You want me to use what I've learned. I can do that by being a good example. Remind me to put to work what You've taught me—to be kind, forgiving, helpful, and honest and to do good works whenever I can. Help me to keep my promises and to always do my best. Let everything I do be a reflection of You. Amen.

MORNING

## Goodness Overcomes Evil

*Be not overcome of evil, but overcome evil with good.*

ROMANS 12:21 KJV

Dear God, all the bad stuff going on in the world makes me angry. You don't want us being mean and doing hateful things. When I see evil fighting good, I think I can't do anything about it. But Romans 12:21 tells me I can. I fight evil by doing good. Your kind of goodness overcomes evil every time. So, Father, I'm ready to join the fight. Help me to spread some goodness around. Amen.

EVENING

## Shun Evil

*Do not be wise in your own eyes; fear the LORD and shun evil. This will bring health to your body and nourishment to your bones.*

PROVERBS 3:7–8 NIV

Heavenly Father, "to shun" means "to send away." Tonight's Bible verse says to shun evil. When I send evil out of my life, You will make me strong. When I follow Your ways instead of my own, You will make me healthy in mind and spirit. Lord, keep evil from entering my heart. Help me to make wise decisions and to use my body in ways that honor You. Amen.

MORNING

## The Fruit of My Mouth

*From the fruit of their mouth a person's stomach is filled; with the harvest of their lips they are satisfied.*

PROVERBS 18:20 NIV

Dear Lord, I hadn't ever thought of my words being like fruit, but I guess they are. Good fruit is sweet and satisfying; people like it and want more. Bad fruit is rotten and smelly. The only place for it is in the garbage. Help my words to be pleasing to others. When I speak, may those listening welcome my words and want to hear what I have to say. Amen.

EVENING

## About Dying

*For as in Adam all die, even so in Christ all shall be made alive.*

1 CORINTHIANS 15:22 NKJV

Dear Jesus, thinking about death is scary. I try not to think about it, but sometimes it creeps into my mind. My pastor said that "Be not afraid" is one of the most repeated commands in the Bible. It's in there over 100 times! So please help me not to be afraid of dying. Everyone dies. When I do someday, I'll be with You—and there's nothing scary about that. You will make heaven my home. Amen.

# DAY 188

## MORNING

# Chosen by Christ

*We were already chosen to be God's own children by Christ. This was done just like the plan He had.*

EPHESIANS 1:11 NLV

Jesus, You were with Your Father when I was created, and You had already chosen me to be a child of God. Even before I was born, You had planned for me to accept You as my Lord and Savior. You planned to forgive all my sins and make a way for me to live with You forever in heaven. Thank You, Jesus, for choosing me to be one of God's children. I love You! Amen.

## EVENING

# A Friend Loves at All Times

*A friend loves at all times.*

PROVERBS 17:17 NKJV

Dear Father God, You've blessed me with lots of friends. I have friends in my neighborhood, at school, at church, on my soccer team—friends all over the place! But do I love them all the time? That's something to think about. I want to show love to all my friends the way You love me: always kind, giving, caring, and forgiving. Help me to be that sort of friend all the time. Amen.

MORNING

# God's Children

*Be ye therefore followers of God, as dear children.*

EPHESIANS 5:1 KJV

Lord, I think it's normal for brothers and sisters to quarrel sometimes. I don't always get along with mine. We fight over dumb, silly things. But You remind me that Your children should be following You, not fighting with each other. So, forgive us, Lord, when we don't get along. Help us to act in ways that please You. I know we will get along even better if we are following Your will. Amen.

EVENING

# God's Commitment to Me

*"Remember his covenant forever—the commitment he made to a thousand generations."*

1 CHRONICLES 16:15 NLT

Heavenly Father, when You created me, You made a commitment to love and care for me forever. You give me everything I need. You take responsibility for me whether I succeed or fail. From the beginning of time, every promise You have made You have kept. And You have never changed. You have made that same commitment to a thousand generations. I want the whole world to know what You've done for me. Amen.

# DAY 190

## MORNING

## Merciful

*Be ye therefore merciful,*
*as your Father also is merciful.*
LUKE 6:36 KJV

Father, I'm thankful for Your gift of mercy—but You know it's not always easy for me to show mercy to others. It's hard for me to be merciful when someone makes the same mistakes with me over and over or does the same wrong thing to me again and again. Father, right now I pray that You'll make me more like You. Help me to show Your mercy to everyone—no matter what.

## EVENING

## Do Not Worry

*Do not worry. Learn to pray about everything. Give thanks*
*to God as you ask Him for what you need. The peace of*
*God is much greater than the human mind can understand.*
*This peace will keep your hearts and minds through Christ Jesus.*
PHILIPPIANS 4:6–7 NLV

Lord, when will I learn that I don't need to worry? Your Word says it's so, and I trust what the Bible tells me. Still, I worry. I worry about stuff at home and at school, and I even worry about what's happening in the world. Remind me to pray and give all my worries to You. Whatever worries me, You have it under control. Give me peace tonight. My faith and trust are in You.

MORNING

# A Cheerful Day

*"Be of good cheer, daughter."*
MATTHEW 9:22 NKJV

I can hear Your words in my heart, Jesus. You're saying, "Be of good cheer, daughter!" I think You enjoyed Your life here on earth, and You want me to enjoy mine too. You want me to have fun today and be cheerful. So let's make this the best day ever. Guide me to try something new. I'm ready for an adventure. Lead me to make some new friends. I'm ready to start the day.

EVENING

# The First Priority

*"'Love the Lord your God with all your heart and with all your soul and with all your mind.' This is the first and greatest commandment."*
MATTHEW 22:37–38 NIV

You should be my first priority, God. Period. Why is that so hard? The day slips by, and I realize I haven't thought much about You. I've made decisions without checking with You. I've said and done things You don't approve of. I know I should put You first before anything else. I need to get better with that, Father. Be a constant reminder. Speak to my heart and shout, "I'm here!" Amen.

MORNING

## Love Your Neighbor

*"And the second [greatest commandment] is like it: 'Love your neighbor as yourself.'"*
MATTHEW 22:39 NIV

Jesus, when I hear the word *neighbor*, I think of the people who live near me. But I think when You said, "Love your neighbor," You meant love everyone. God is love, and He wants us to share His love with everyone we meet. That means being kind, caring, and forgiving. Help me to discover new ways to show my neighbors that I love them. Guide me to be good to them like You are.

EVENING

## Ministering to Others

*"But rise and stand on your feet; for I have appeared to you for this purpose, to make you a minister and a witness."*
ACTS 26:16 NKJV

Father, a minister is someone who teaches about You. I hadn't thought of myself as a minister, but I guess that whenever I tell a friend about You and Jesus, that's what I am. I like sharing what I've learned about You with others. When I speak about You, help me to always speak the truth. Let the Bible be my guide. I'd like my purpose to be sharing You with everyone I meet. Amen.

MORNING

## Faith Is My Shield

*Above all, taking the shield of faith, wherewith ye shall be able to quench all the fiery darts of the wicked.*

EPHESIANS 6:16 KJV

Heavenly Father, my faith in You is my shield. It is that strong force that protects me from evil. When someone tries to hurt me with their words or by doing mean things to me, I have faith that You are my shield and protector. Make my faith in You strong. Lord, help me to believe so much in Your amazing power that nothing will ever get between You and me. Amen.

EVENING

## Nobody's Perfect

*Make allowance for each other's faults, and forgive anyone who offends you. Remember, the Lord forgave you, so you must forgive others.*

COLOSSIANS 3:13 NLT

Dear God, thanks for reminding me through tonight's Bible verse that I'm not perfect, and neither are my friends and family. We all mess up sometimes. Forgiveness doesn't come easily, but it should. You forgive me all the time, so I should be just as forgiving toward those who hurt me. Help me to remember that we all have faults. Lead me to be more understanding and forgiving. Amen.

MORNING

# It's Simple

*[Paul and Silas] replied, "Believe in the Lord Jesus, and you will be saved—you and your household."*

ACTS 16:31 NIV

Dear Jesus, I know I will never be perfect like You are. Even when I try my best to please You, I mess up sometimes. Before You came, people tried to find ways to be good enough to get into heaven. But You made it simple. Your message is "Believe in Me and be saved from sin." Such a simple message but such a great reward.

EVENING

# The Way of Peace

*The fruit of that righteousness will be peace; its effect will be quietness and confidence forever.*

ISAIAH 32:17 NIV

Father, when I do my best to follow Your ways, I will find peace. Peace is in the quiet times You and I spend together. During those times, You strengthen me, comfort me, and remind me of how much You love and care for me. The time I spend with You gives me confidence that there's nothing You and I can't do together. And that adds to my peace. Thank You, God. Amen.

MORNING

## God's Gentleness

*Thou hast also given me the shield of thy salvation: and thy gentleness hath made me great.*

2 SAMUEL 22:36 KJV

Dear God, how can You be so huge and powerful and yet so very gentle? The Bible says You watch over small things. Not one sparrow falls to the ground without You seeing. You watch over us like a shepherd caring for His sheep. The Bible says if even one sheep is lost, You go looking for it and bring it back. You are my great, powerful, and gentle God, and I love You. Amen.

EVENING

## New Heart and Mind

*Let your minds and hearts be made new. You must become a new person and be God-like. Then you will be made right with God and have a true holy life.*

EPHESIANS 4:23–24 NLV

Lord, slowly I'm becoming new in my heart and mind. When I choose to follow You instead of going my own way, I become more like You. When I forgive people or show goodness toward them, I'm acting like You would. Continue to help me grow to be more like You. I want to be thinking about You and Your will all the time. I want my heart to be a reflection of Yours. Amen.

DAY 196

MORNING

# Quiet and Gentle

*The unfading beauty of a gentle and quiet spirit*
*. . .is of great worth in God's sight.*

1 PETER 3:4 NIV

Dear God, I can be loud sometimes—loud and not so nice. That's not how I want to be. Will You help me to have a quieter and gentler spirit? It's okay to be loud when I'm playing or cheering at a game. But yelling at my siblings isn't right. The Bible says a gentle, quiet spirit is beautiful and of great worth to You. That's the kind of spirit I want. Amen.

EVENING

# The Right Time

*People can make all kinds of plans,*
*but only the LORD's plan will happen.*

PROVERBS 19:21 NCV

Father God, there's so much I want to do, but I just don't know when to do it. Your timing is everything. You know the steps I need to take and when to get moving. I ask You to lead and guide me. Help me to know when it's time to step forward. Then walk with me all along the way. Thank You for making everything happen in Your time, not mine. Amen.

MORNING

## God's Armor

*But since we belong to the day, let us be sober,*
*putting on faith and love as a breastplate,*
*and the hope of salvation as a helmet.*

1 THESSALONIANS 5:8 NIV

My heavenly Father, as I begin this day, remind me to put on Your armor. Shield my heart with Your faithfulness and love. Protect my mind with the helmet of salvation. This is Your reminder to protect my thoughts and keep them centered on Jesus. Give me Your power to fight whenever trouble tries to get in my way today. Lead me and guide me in the way I should go. Amen.

EVENING

## Remember

*He has made His wonderful works to be remembered;*
*the LORD is gracious and full of compassion.*

PSALM 111:4 NKJV

Dear Lord, when I feel sad or when things don't go my way, help me to remember all the wonderful things You do for me. Remind me of how beautiful life can be. Open my eyes to the goodness around me, and set my thoughts on Your never-ending goodness. Lift me up above my feelings of sadness and frustration, and give me a heart that's cheerful, grateful, and glad. Amen.

MORNING

## Everlasting Love

*The LORD appeared to him long ago, saying,*
*"I have loved you with an everlasting love;*
*therefore I have drawn you out with kindness."*
JEREMIAH 31:3 NASB

Dear Father, I have a daily to-do list. Often, instead of praising You for what I accomplish, I get upset with myself for not doing even more. I try my best to please You. But today You're reminding me I don't need to earn Your approval by my good works. I can never do enough to earn Your love. You already love me completely and forever, and nothing I do will change that.

EVENING

## Not What I Expected

*Let us hold tightly without wavering to the hope we*
*affirm, for God can be trusted to keep his promise.*
HEBREWS 10:23 NLT

Lord, I expected things to work out differently, and I'm so disappointed. Help me to accept that You are in control and that what I want might not be what You want for me. Take my disappointment. Help me let it go. You are faithful. You keep Your promises. It's enough today that You promise to always give me exactly what I need when I need it. You had other plans for me, and that's all right.

MORNING

## A Quiet Strength

*"In quietness and confidence shall be your strength."*

ISAIAH 30:15 NKJV

Lord, when I face problems, I often feel I don't have enough strength to solve them. But if I go to You and pray, You give me strength. You provide me with confidence to make the best decisions about all my problems. When I need confidence and strength, will You whisper in my heart, "Come to Me"? And if I don't listen, God, shout it to me. You are my confidence and my strength! Amen.

EVENING

## My Eyes Are on the Crown

*My eyes are on the crown. I want to win the race and get the crown of God's call from heaven through Christ Jesus.*

PHILIPPIANS 3:14 NLV

God, Your follower Paul wrote tonight's Bible verse. The crown is the reward he will receive in heaven for doing Your work here on earth. His goal was to do so well that You would honor him when he arrived in heaven. I'd like that to be my goal too. Help me to do my best so that when I meet You face-to-face, You will tell me how proud You are of me. Amen.

MORNING

## Be Prepared

*"Be ready and dressed. Have your lights burning."*

Luke 12:35 NLV

Heavenly Father, sin is always ready to fool me, to knock me off the path that leads to You. This morning's verse reminds me to be watchful and ready. Open my eyes to the sin that's all around me. Keep me from falling for its tricks. Give me all the weapons I need to be strong and stand against it. With You on my side, I'm ready and safe. Amen.

EVENING

## Tell It to Jesus

*If we confess our sins, he is faithful and just and will forgive us our sins and purify us from all unrighteousness.*

1 John 1:9 NIV

Dear Jesus, I'm sorry. Those two words are hard to say when I know I've given in to sin. I put off praying. I don't want to come to You and confess that I messed up. I would rather have behaved in a way that made You proud. But I know You will forgive me. You always do. So, Jesus, I'm sorry. I will try again to do better next time. Amen.

MORNING

## Wide Awake

*Therefore let us not sleep, as do others;*
*but let us watch and be sober.*

1 THESSALONIANS 5:6 KJV

You know how tired I am, God. I'm in the middle of a big project. Most of it hasn't been easy. I've had to back up a few times and start over. Help me not to allow my tiredness to lead to feeling frustrated and discouraged. Send people to encourage me and help me reach my goal. Keep me wide awake and alert, focused always on You. Thank You, Father. Amen.

EVENING

## See It Through

*The way of the good person is like the light of dawn,*
*growing brighter and brighter until full daylight.*

PROVERBS 4:18 NCV

Dear Lord, this project isn't turning out as I thought it would. I've had problems, it seems, at every turn. You never said it would be easy, but You promised to help me do more than I can imagine. Help me to see this project through to the end. Show me what it looks like through Your eyes. Then help me make Your vision a reality. Amen.

MORNING

## Call on the Lord

*"I will call on the name of the Lord. The God Who answers by fire, He is God." All the people answered and said, "That is a good idea."*

1 KINGS 18:24 NLV

Dear Lord, there is never a time I call out to You and You aren't instantly listening. You are never too busy to hear me. You know even before I call on You that I need You. If I think You are silent, remind me that You are always with me. You know what I need before I even ask. Help is just a prayer away. I am never alone. Amen.

EVENING

## Morning, Noon, and Night

*Listen to my voice in the morning, LORD.*
*Each morning I bring my requests to you and wait expectantly.*

PSALM 5:3 NLT

Lord God, every morning I come to You. I ask for Your help throughout the day. All day long, I feel You with me. You encourage me. You give me strength. And You even give me a little friendly nudge when I'm afraid to try something new. At night when I pray, I thank You for all You have done. You are my God, and You are good to me. Amen.

MORNING

## A Safe Place on High

*Because he has loved Me, I will bring him out of trouble. I will set him in a safe place on high, because he has known My name.*

PSALM 91:14 NLV

Dear God, because I trust You to always lead me out of trouble, I'm not worried or afraid. If fear tries to sneak into my heart, all I need to do is call Your name. Your love will overcome any fear that tries to reach me. You are my safe place, my God on high in heaven. You rule heaven and earth, and nothing—*nothing at all*—makes You afraid. Fear is afraid of You!

EVENING

## Encouragement

*May our Lord Jesus Christ himself and God our Father, who loved us and by his grace gave us eternal encouragement and good hope, encourage your hearts and strengthen you in every good deed and word.*

2 THESSALONIANS 2:16–17 NIV

Father God and Lord Jesus, I need encouragement. Tomorrow is a big day for me with big challenges. Will You please bring me peace tonight and strengthen me? Lead me tomorrow in all I say and do. I need You to lift my spirit and help me soar. Let me be like an eagle that glides on the wind, courageous, strong, and confident. We can do this! We've got this. Amen.

# DAY 204

## MORNING

# Rejoice and Be Glad!

*This is the day the LORD has made;*
*we will rejoice and be glad in it.*
PSALM 118:24 NKJV

Dear God, I'm sure You have many blessings waiting for me this day. The first blessing of today is You created it. You made this day, and You already have it planned for me. Just knowing that makes me glad. I'm rejoicing that You have this great day all ready for me. I can't wait to see where You will take me and what new things I'll learn.

## EVENING

# Overflowing Love

*We give thanks to the God and Father of our Lord Jesus Christ. He is our Father Who shows us loving-kindness and our God Who gives us comfort.*
2 CORINTHIANS 1:3 NLV

Dear heavenly Father, You love us so much. Fill up my heart with Your love. I want Your love inside my heart to overflow to others. Teach me how to share it with them. Show me what I can give of myself to others to make their lives better or to bring them comfort and peace. Open my eyes to the needs around me, and then give me ideas about how I can help. Amen.

MORNING

## God Takes Care of Me

*The Lord takes care of all who love Him.*

PSALM 145:20 NLV

Dear God, wherever I go, I trust You to take care of me. You will protect me. I might not feel You with me. It might not be obvious that You are taking care of me. But I'm sure that You are. You've promised to take care of everyone who loves You—and I love You. Wherever I am, You are with me, watching over me and using Your power to keep me safe. Amen.

EVENING

## Stay True to God

*We think of those who stayed true to Him as happy even though they suffered. You have heard how long Job waited. You have seen what the Lord did for him in the end. The Lord is full of loving-kindness and pity.*

JAMES 5:11 NLV

God, I've read the story of Job in the Bible. He suffered a lot, but he never gave up on You. He waited a long time before his suffering went away; but in the end, You blessed him with even more than he had before his trouble started. Father, help me to stay true to You. Whatever trouble comes my way, help me not to give up. I know You will bring me through it.

DAY 206

MORNING

# Someone Lied to Me

*If we confess our sins, he is faithful and just to forgive us our sins, and to cleanse us from all unrighteousness.*

1 John 1:9 KJV

Dear God, a friend lied to me yesterday. It was a little lie, but it felt like a big one to me. I trusted my friend to tell the truth. It's been on my mind since then. What she did was wrong, but I do things that displease You too. Neither of us is perfect. We both do things we're ashamed of. Will You help us both to do better? Amen.

EVENING

# Bless My Enemies

*Wish good for those who harm you; wish them well and do not curse them.*

Romans 12:14 NCV

Heavenly Father, I pray that You will bless those who have not been kind to me. You know who they are. I want to forgive them the way You always forgive me. Sometimes I feel like I just want to get back at them. But that isn't what You want me to do. Give me strength to be kind to them and even helpful. Bless them, Lord, and bless me too. Amen.

MORNING

## My Temporary Home

*They agreed that they were foreigners and nomads here on earth. Obviously people who say such things are looking forward to a country they can call their own.*

HEBREWS 11:13–14 NLT

Dear God, this is my home. I can't imagine living anywhere else, especially living somewhere other than earth. But You want me to remember that earth is my temporary home. You have a forever home waiting for me when my time is done here. Heaven is a real place, a wonderful place! While You want me to enjoy every minute on earth, You want me to keep my thoughts turned toward heaven and You.

EVENING

## Let's All Work Together

*Make me truly happy by agreeing wholeheartedly with each other, loving one another, and working together with one mind and purpose.*

PHILIPPIANS 2:2 NLT

Father God, great things happen when people work together. Teamwork gets things done. A team that works well together wins the game. What if everyone on earth worked together to get Your work done? I can imagine all earth's people working together, loving one another, and having the same goal and purpose—to please You. What a wonderful world that would be. It sounds a lot like heaven, doesn't it?

MORNING

# I'm Satisfied with What I Have

*I will be fully satisfied as with the richest of foods;*
*with singing lips my mouth will praise you.*

PSALM 63:5 NIV

Heavenly Father, You have given me so many good things. Still, I often want more. Setting goals is a good thing. It's good to want more learning, more talent, more skills, more friends. But when it comes to more toys, games, and electronics—do I really need those things? Help me to be forever grateful for what I have and to want more of what pleases You. Amen.

EVENING

# Out of This World

*We do not use those things to fight with that the world uses. We use the things God gives to fight with and they have power. Those things God gives to fight with destroy the strong-places of the devil.*

2 CORINTHIANS 10:4 NLV

Mighty God, when trouble gets in my way and makes me afraid, You give me all the weapons I need to fight it. Your weapons aren't of this world. They aren't guns, knives, and other worldly weapons. Your weapons are faith and trust. When I put my faith and trust in You, You promise me strength to battle whatever is in my way. Better yet, You will lead me in the fight, and You always win.

MORNING

## God's Promises

*The LORD will preserve him, and keep him alive; and he shall be blessed upon the earth: and thou wilt not deliver him unto the will of his enemies.*

PSALM 41:2 KJV

Father, the Bible is full of Your promises. They aren't just "sometimes" promises. They are for everyone reading Your Word and for all time. You promise to take care of me no matter what danger I might face. You promise me a forever home in heaven. While I live on earth, You promise to bless me and protect me from my enemies. Lord, I trust in Your promises, and I trust in You. Amen.

EVENING

## Light of the World

*"You are the light of the world—like a city on a hilltop that cannot be hidden."*

MATTHEW 5:14 NLT

Jesus, You said those who believe in You are the light of the world. We bring light into the world by sharing the good news—that You came to save us from sin and give us forever life in heaven. When people hear about You and believe, then You bring their souls out of the dark place where they are living without You. You fill up their hearts with the bright light of Your love.

MORNING

# God Is Perfection

*As for God, His way is perfect.*
2 SAMUEL 22:31 AMPC

Father, I can only define *perfect* through my earthly eyes. When I get all the answers right on a test, that's perfect. Or when my team shuts out the other, not allowing them to score, that's perfect. Your kind of perfect is different. It's beyond anything I can understand. Although I don't always understand Your ways, I know they are faultless. Why? Because You're perfect! Everything You are, and everything You do, will never fail.

EVENING

# Blessed!

*"Blessed are those whose transgressions are forgiven, whose sins are covered."*
ROMANS 4:7 NIV

Dear Jesus, how blessed I am to have my sins forgiven! You must love me so much to have died for me. You put all of my sin on Yourself, and then You got rid of it forever. Thanks to You, I don't have to earn a place in heaven. It's already there waiting for me. Thank You for Your gift of forgiveness. And please help me to be more forgiving toward others. Amen.

MORNING

## Kept Forever

*For the Lord loves what is fair and right. He does not leave the people alone who belong to Him. They are kept forever.*

PSALM 37:28 NLV

Father God, forever is an idea that's hard to imagine. Everything here on earth has a beginning and an end. It's all about time. I wonder, does time exist in heaven? Is it the same as here on earth? I have belonged to You since even before You created me, and I will belong to You forever. On days when I feel alone, help me to remember that. Amen.

EVENING

## Be Thoughtful

*Don't act thoughtlessly, but understand what the Lord wants you to do.*

EPHESIANS 5:17 NLT

Lord, will You please help me to be more understanding of what others need? Sometimes I pass off my parents' grumpiness as just them being, well, grown-ups! But maybe they're grumpy because they had a bad day at work. I want to be more thoughtful. Help me to be more aware of how others are feeling, and then guide my thoughts to do what I can to help them feel better. Thank You. Amen.

MORNING

## Just Do It

*But be doers of the word, and not hearers only, deceiving yourselves.*
JAMES 1:22 NKJV

Dear heavenly Father, I'm learning from reading the Bible and the scripture verses in this book how You expect me to behave. I know the Ten Commandments. I've read many of Your other instructions for behaving right. But I'm sorry to say, I don't always do what the Bible says. I'm going to try harder, God. When I slip up and go my own way, will You remind me? Amen.

EVENING

## Clothed in Compassion

*Therefore, as God's chosen people, holy and dearly loved, clothe yourselves with compassion, kindness, humility, gentleness and patience.*
COLOSSIANS 3:12 NIV

Dear God, if there were an outfit called *Compassion*, it would be made from the finest materials: kindness, gentleness, patience, and humility. It would be simply beautiful—not at all bright and flashy to draw attention. Instead, it would look like the most comfortable outfit anyone would ever want to put on. You are the designer, God. I'm ready to model Your creation. Clothe me in compassion. Amen.

MORNING

## Saved from All Evil

*The LORD shall preserve thee from all evil:*
*he shall preserve thy soul.*
PSALM 121:7 KJV

Father God, evil comes in so many shapes and forms. Sometimes it comes into my life disguised, and by the time I recognize its presence, my soul is already in danger of being tricked into doing things that won't please You. When this happens, Father, be my rescuer (even when I don't ask for rescuing!). Thank You, Lord, that You are always watching over me—and You will protect me from evil of every kind.

EVENING

## My Best

*"Be bold and diligent. And GOD be*
*with you as you do your best."*
2 CHRONICLES 19:11 MSG

Jesus, gentle shepherd, I want to do my best, knowing that You are with me all the way. Help me to be brave. Help me not to panic or be anxious about anything. I need to focus on You. Please build up my faith and confidence. Keep me on track. I'm ready to listen to Your voice, Jesus. Lead me where You want me to go, and I will follow You. Amen.

DAY 214

MORNING

# My Hiding Place

*Thou art my hiding place; thou shalt preserve me from trouble; thou shalt compass me about with songs of deliverance.*

Psalm 32:7 KJV

God, when I was little, hiding and jumping out at my brother was fun. Hiding can be a game. But some days I feel like hiding to get away from stuff that bothers me. I want to go somewhere quiet where I can just chill. You are my quiet place, God. When I'm alone talking with You, I feel safe and strong. Nothing can get to me whenever I'm with You. Amen.

EVENING

# Ready for Anything

*I have strength for all things in Christ Who empowers me [I am ready for anything and equal to anything through Him Who infuses inner strength into me; I am self-sufficient in Christ's sufficiency].*

Philippians 4:13 AMPC

Dear Lord Jesus, with Your strength and power backing me, I'm ready for anything! When Your power gives my confidence a boost, I do things I thought I couldn't. If I feel tired and my energy is gone or when I feel like giving up, You empower me to keep going. Thank You for walking with me all through the day and helping me with all that I do. Amen.

MORNING

# I Rely on God's Word

*I lean on, rely on, and trust in Your word.*
PSALM 119:42 AMPC

Dear God, I'm in a hurry most mornings, and sometimes I don't start my day reading the Bible. Your Word is the best way to get a head start on my day. Reading even a little before I go to school helps me to stay focused on You. I trust in the Bible to teach and guide me. Please remind me to start each day reading from Your Word. Amen.

EVENING

# Know-It-All

*Don't try to impress others. Be humble, thinking of others as better than yourselves.*
PHILIPPIANS 2:3 NLT

I'm guilty, God. Sometimes I try to impress others with how much I know. I'm always ready to give advice to my little brothers and sisters. I tell them how I think they should do things. Sometimes they tell me, "Stop being so bossy!" Will You help me not to be a know-it-all? I catch myself being one, and I try to stop. But sometimes the words just slip past my lips. Amen.

DAY 216

MORNING

# Minding My Own Business

*Aspire to lead a quiet life, to mind your own business, and to work with your own hands.*

1 Thessalonians 4:11 NKJV

Father, at a sleepover, we talked about a girl in our class. Some things we said weren't very nice. I don't know this girl well, and what she does really isn't any of my business. I want to remember to be quiet before I say something mean or hurtful. I need to stay out of other people's business. Lord, help my words to be kind and my thoughts to be set on what's good. Amen.

EVENING

# Paths of Righteousness

*All the paths of the Lord are loving and true for those who keep His agreement and keep His Laws.*

Psalm 25:10 NLV

Lord, I learned Psalm 23 in Sunday school. I memorized it. Some of its words are "He leadeth me in the paths of righteousness for his name's sake"(verse 3 KJV). It means You lead us on the path of right living because it brings honor to Your name. Father, the path of righteousness is loving and true. If I follow Your commands and walk where You lead me, I know I can't go wrong. Amen.

MORNING

## Hurt Feelings

*He is my God, my rock, where I go to be safe.*
*He is my covering and the horn that saves me, my strong place where I go to be safe. You save me from being hurt.*
2 SAMUEL 22:3 NLV

Father God, You save me from being hurt. As I've learned to put my faith and trust in You, I've discovered that it takes a lot for someone to hurt my feelings. You've taught me to forgive those who hurt me, to pray for them, and to try to understand that maybe they didn't mean to hurt me. When my feelings get hurt, I run to You and You make it all better. Amen.

EVENING

## Shelter in Him

*Those who live in the shelter of the Most High will find rest in the shadow of the Almighty.*
PSALM 91:1 NLT

Dear heavenly Father, when it's raining and storming outside, I'm even more grateful for the shelter of my home where I'm comfortable, safe, and dry. You are my shelter too. When trouble rains down on me, You are the one who covers and protects me. I feel safe in Your shadow, knowing that nothing can harm me. Shelter me tonight, God. Cover me with Your love while I rest. Amen.

# DAY 218

MORNING

## Let It Be So

*I will praise You, for I am fearfully and wonderfully made.*

Psalm 139:14 NKJV

Father, my family has been working on a hard jigsaw puzzle. It's taking forever to figure out where all the pieces go. When I think of how easy it is for You to create a person, I'm reminded of Your greatness. Our bodies have so many parts, some so tiny they can't be seen. You're not puzzled putting us together. You just say, "Let it be so," and all the parts fit perfectly.

EVENING

## Loving Favor

*Loving-favor has been given to each one of us.*
*We can see how great it is by the gift of Christ.*

Ephesians 4:7 NLV

Dear Jesus, every day You give me just the right amount of loving favor. You show me that You love me by meeting all my needs. You help me all through the day. You give me strength to do what I think I can't, and You protect me when trouble gets in my way. You stay with me, always watching over me. Then at night You give me rest. Thank You for loving me, Jesus. Amen.

MORNING

## Thanks for What I Have

*Keep your lives free from the love of money and be content with what you have.*

HEBREWS 13:5 NIV

Dear God, ads are everywhere. Makeup, clothes, hair products, toys, games, phones. . . Ads make people want things. They make people want more. Wanting more stuff isn't what You desire for me. You want me to find joy in You and all the ways You bless me. You don't bless me so I can be selfish. Instead, You want me to be grateful for what I have. I *am* grateful, Lord. Thank You. Amen.

EVENING

## Worldly Fears

*"Blessed is the one who trusts in the LORD, whose confidence is in him."*

JEREMIAH 17:7 NIV

"What are you afraid of?" That was a question in my youth group on Sunday. I answered, "Spiders." God, some kids had bigger fears about things happening in their families and in the world. Our pastor reminded us that whatever we're afraid of, whether it's something little or big, we can trust You to protect us. You are bigger and way more powerful than any fearful thing in the world. You are almighty God.

MORNING

# My Refuge

*The Lord also will be a refuge for the oppressed, a refuge in times of trouble.*

Psalm 9:9 KJV

Father, *refuge* was a word I needed to look up. It means a place of peace, love, and acceptance. You are my refuge in times of trouble. When problems press down on me and I need protection, I can always run to You. I like knowing that whatever happens, You are my safe place. And I don't have to go far to find You because You are always with me, right here in my heart. Amen.

EVENING

# Giving Forgiveness

*"If you forgive other people when they sin against you, your heavenly Father will also forgive you."*

Matthew 6:14 NIV

Heavenly Father, because You have forgiven me, You also expect me to forgive others. How can I hold on to being angry with others while knowing that You forgive me for every wrong thing I do? You want Your forgiveness to be an example of how I treat others. Help me to forgive anyone who is mean to me or hurts my feelings. Help me to love them as You have loved me. Amen.

MORNING

## Where's Your Missing Piece?

*In Him you have been made complete.*

COLOSSIANS 2:10 NASB

Dear God, people who don't know You are like a puzzle missing a piece. They're incomplete. I want to tell others about You, but I'm uncertain who needs to hear and how I should tell them. I need Your eyes, Lord. Help me to see who needs You. Then give me just the right words at the right time to tell them about You. Come into their hearts. Make them whole and complete. Amen.

EVENING

## God's Control

*Blessed are those whose help is the God of Jacob, whose hope is in the LORD their God. He is the Maker of heaven and earth, the sea, and everything in them—he remains faithful forever.*

PSALM 146:5–6 NIV

Sometimes I look up at the sky and I say, "Wow, God made that!" Oceans, mountains, flowers and trees, animals and people—You made them all. Every detail is just perfect; everything fits together according to Your will. You control all things in this world and beyond. Thank You, God, for being faithful to us and for making this world that we live in. Thank You for loving us and helping us every day.

## DAY 222

MORNING

# Managing My Time

*Teach us to number our days,*
*that we may gain a heart of wisdom.*
PSALM 90:12 NIV

Father, I waste time. I get busy playing games, watching TV, and listening to music; and before I know it, I haven't accomplished anything. Then I rush around trying to do what has to get done. I want to manage my time better. Will You be my reminder? When I make good use of my time, I know it pleases You. Help me use my time to learn and to grow nearer to You. Amen.

EVENING

# I Won't Be Discouraged!

*The LORD makes firm the steps of the one who delights in him; though he may stumble, he will not fall, for the LORD upholds him with his hand.*
PSALM 37:23–24 NIV

Dear God, I get frustrated when I try to accomplish something and fail. My parents tell me not to be so hard on myself and to keep trying. But when I try and fail, it feels like falling flat on my face. Tonight's verse reminds me that when I fall, You are the one who picks me up. I'm not going to be discouraged! Instead, I'll put my faith in You, get up, and try again.

MORNING

# A Song in My Heart

*I will sing of thy power; yea, I will sing aloud of thy mercy in the morning: for thou hast been my defence and refuge in the day of my trouble.*

Psalm 59:16 KJV

Heavenly Father, I'm going to begin today with a song in my heart. Give me a song to remind me of Your power and love. Let that song stay with me wherever I go. Make it a joyful song, a song that reminds me that whatever problems or troubles I face, You've already taken them from me and they're in Your control. Today I sing praises to You, God, because You are so good to me.

EVENING

# My Savior

*"He is the one all the prophets testified about, saying that everyone who believes in him will have their sins forgiven through his name."*

Acts 10:43 NLT

Jesus, You are my Savior. I don't ever want to overlook all You've done for me. It's no little thing that You suffered and died so my sins will be forgiven. It's huge that You love me so much You would give Your life for me. People hated You. They beat You, embarrassed You, and killed You in the worst possible way. Don't ever let me forget that. Thank You, Jesus, my Savior and my God.

DAY 224

MORNING

## Hope in God's Word

*Thou art my hiding place and my shield: I hope in thy word.*

PSALM 119:114 KJV

God, I find hope when I read my Bible and think about Your words. The Bible reminds me of how much You love me. It's one way that I connect with You. When I read, the words are for me. You are speaking directly to me. I know You have amazing plans for me. You are my hope for the future. Lead me and guide me, Father, as I spend time reading Your Word. Amen.

EVENING

## Loving-Kindness to All

*"The loving-kindness of the Lord is given to the people of all times who honor Him."*

LUKE 1:50 NLV

Father God, from the beginning, You have shown loving-kindness to those who honor You. Even when Your people messed up and went the wrong way, You led them back to You. From generation to generation, You have remained faithful even when Your people doubted You. When they came back to You and honored You, You showered them with loving-kindness. It was true then, and it's true today. I honor You, God, and I thank You.

MORNING

## I Prayed for You

*As he prays for you, he asks God to help you to be strong and to make you perfect. He prays that you will know what God wants you to do in all things.*

COLOSSIANS 4:12 NLV

I thank You, God, for all the people who have faithfully prayed for me. I know some of them; but others have prayed for me, and I don't even know their names. Bless them today. Meet all their needs and give them strength. Keep them safe in the shelter of Your love. Who else should I pray for today, Lord? Bring them into my mind, and give me the words to pray. Amen.

EVENING

## Sneak Attack

*The Lord is faithful, who will establish you and guard you from the evil one.*

2 THESSALONIANS 3:3 NKJV

Dear Father God, sin is so sneaky. It's always waiting around the next corner, trying to get me to fall into its trap. It wants me to say and do things that displease You. It loves when I hurt someone's feelings or disappoint them when they need my help. Please, Father, help me to stay on guard for those sneak attacks. Protect me and lead me far from sin. Amen.

MORNING

## Evil in the World

*"I do not ask You to take them out of the world.*
*I ask You to keep them from the devil."*
JOHN 17:15 NLV

Dear Lord Jesus, I know there are evil people in the world doing evil things. I think the world would be a better place without them. But maybe a better thing would be for me to pray for them. Jesus, please work on their hearts. Get them to leave their evil ways and instead follow You. That might seem impossible, Lord. But with You all things are possible. Amen.

EVENING

## Role Models

*Look at the man without blame. And watch the man who is right and good. For the man of peace will have much family to follow him.*
PSALM 37:37 NLV

Dear Jesus, You are the best of role models. You are completely without blame and perfect in every way. Everything You did when You were here on earth was right and good. I know if I try to be like You, I will find peace in my heart. And if I become like You, then I will be a good role model for others. Teach me, Jesus. I'm ready. Amen.

MORNING

## Face in the Mirror

*All of us, with no covering on our faces, show the shining-greatness of the Lord as in a mirror. All the time we are being changed to look like Him, with more and more of His shining-greatness.*

2 CORINTHIANS 3:18 NLV

God, when I look in the mirror, what do I see? You want me to see a girl who is God's child. . .a girl who looks up to her heavenly Father for guidance . . .a girl who is becoming more like her Father every day. That's my goal, Lord—to become so much like You that when I look in the mirror, my face reflects Your goodness and love. Help me, Father, to become *that* girl.

EVENING

## So Simple?

*For God so loved the world that he gave his one and only Son, that whoever believes in him shall not perish but have eternal life.*

JOHN 3:16 NIV

Can it be so simple, Jesus? I only have to believe? You promised my faith in You will open the door for me to have forever life in heaven one day. I don't have to earn my place there. You've made it so my place is already waiting for me. You gave Your life so all who believe can spend forever with You. Thank You, Jesus. I never want to be separated from You.

MORNING

# Maybe?

*"Let your yes be YES. Let your no be NO. Anything more than this comes from the devil."*

MATTHEW 5:37 NLV

Jesus, did You really mean that if I answer "maybe" instead of "yes" or "no," it comes from the devil? I guess uncertainty isn't good, but if I come to You and ask, You will always help me choose right from wrong. I think You meant I should be true to my word and keep my promises. "Yes" means yes. "No" means no. Make me a person others can trust. Amen.

EVENING

# Overcoming Mountains

*Truly I tell you, whoever says to this mountain, Be lifted up and thrown into the sea! and does not doubt at all in his heart but believes that what he says will take place, it will be done for him.*

MARK 11:23 AMPC

Dear Jesus, the mountains in my life aren't made of rock. They're everyday things like trying my best in school and at sports and dealing with people who aren't nice to me. I've built a mountain of doubt and fear. I cast it now into the sea. No mountain is too big for You. If I put all my faith in You, I can overcome any obstacle that gets in my way.

MORNING

## What If I Run Out?

*"Whoever drinks the water I give them will never thirst. Indeed, the water I give them will become in them a spring of water welling up to eternal life."*
JOHN 4:14 NIV

Heavenly Father, sometimes I worry that I won't have enough. Enough courage. Enough strength. Enough energy. Enough forgiveness. Enough faith. When I feel like I'm running out of anything, I know I can count on Your Holy Spirit inside me to spring up and refill my supply. You are like a well that never runs dry. Thank You for supplying all that I need. Amen.

EVENING

## Hard Work

*She sees that what she has earned is good.*
*Her lamp does not go out at night.*
PROVERBS 31:18 NLV

I did it, God! I worked really hard, and it paid off. When I reached the finish line, I came in first. Thank You for giving me all I needed. You gave me energy to work long and hard. You gave me courage and confidence. And when I won, You gave me humility. I didn't take all the credit for myself. Instead, I said I couldn't have done it without You. Thanks, God, for everything!

MORNING

## Mark a Straight Path

*Mark out a straight path for your feet so that those who are weak and lame will not fall but become strong.*

HEBREWS 12:13 NLT

Heavenly Father, I want to be a strong leader. I want to mark a straight path for others to follow. That means setting a good example. If I follow Your path, then those following me will walk in my footsteps. Along the way, they'll learn more about You. Let me be that kind of example for my younger brothers and sisters and for my friends. Allow me to lead them into a good life with You. Amen.

EVENING

## Jesus, My Friend

*"You are My friends if you do what I command you."*

JOHN 15:14 NASB

Lord Jesus, how do I show that I'm Your friend? You tell me in tonight's Bible verse: *obedience*. When I follow Your commands, I'm showing that I love You. When I put Your commands into action, I prove my faithfulness. When I trust You to help in times of trouble, I'm drawn nearer to You and our friendship is strengthened. Help me to be obedient, Lord. Guide me. You are my very best friend. Amen.

MORNING

## Time Machine

*There is a time for everything, and a season for every activity under the heavens.*

ECCLESIASTES 3:1 NIV

Dear God, I have so much to do and so little time. I always feel like I'm running behind. I know this isn't what You want. Jesus was never in a hurry. He had time to pray on a mountainside, chat beside a well, sit by a lake, and cook fish with friends. Help me to be wiser about my time, and remind me to always make time for You. Amen.

EVENING

## For the Poor and Needy

*"When you give to the needy, do not let your left hand know what your right hand is doing, so that your giving may be in secret. Then your Father, who sees what is done in secret, will reward you."*

MATTHEW 6:3–4 NIV

Lord God, I pray tonight for the poor and needy. Please provide food and shelter to meet their needs. Keep them safe in Your care. Lead them to people who will share the good news about Jesus with them. Please fill their hearts with Your love. Show me how I can help them, Lord. What can I do right here in my community to help meet their needs? Amen.

DAY 232

MORNING

# Be Ready

*Get your minds ready for good use. Keep awake. Set your hope now and forever on the loving-favor to be given you when Jesus Christ comes again.*

1 Peter 1:13 NLV

Jesus, You are coming back to earth someday. The Bible says it's so. We don't know when, but You're coming to do away with evil forever and to make everything perfect and right, the way God planned for it to be. The job of all Christians is to be ready by staying true to You and to make others ready by sharing the good news about You. Make me ready, Lord. I want to serve You.

EVENING

# I Praise Him for Strength

*To You, O my Strength, I will sing praises; for God is my defense, my God of mercy.*

Psalm 59:17 NKJV

Dear God, I praise You tonight for giving me strength. It was my first day at a new school, and I was really nervous. But You gave me strength to get through the day one step at a time. Everything is unfamiliar right now, but I'm sure that before long I'll fit right in. And thanks, God, for the new people I met today. I think we're going to be great friends. Amen.

MORNING

# Hospitality

*Use hospitality one to another without grudging.*

1 PETER 4:9 KJV

Dear Jesus, people often showed You hospitality. They invited You into their homes. The Bible talks about times You visited the home of Your friends Mary and Martha. Entertaining others is a good way not only to have good times together but also to tell others about You. When I invite my friends over, show me ways I can bring You into our activities and conversation. Thanks, Lord. Amen.

EVENING

# Praise to the Creator

*Bless the LORD, O my soul! O LORD my God, You are very great: You are clothed with honor and majesty, who cover Yourself with light as with a garment, who stretch out the heavens like a curtain.*

PSALM 104:1–2 NKJV

Dear heavenly Father, Creator of heaven and earth, You made the planets, the stars, the water, and the land where I am right now. You created every living thing. Tonight's Bible verse says You are covered in light. Your greatness stretches all across the heavens like a curtain. I can feel the light of Your loving-kindness, Father. It's all around me. In Your presence, I praise Your holy name. Amen.

# DAY 234

MORNING

## Faithful

*The Lord is faithful, who shall stablish you, and keep you from evil.*

2 THESSALONIANS 3:3 KJV

Dear Lord, You are always faithful to me. When I show faith in You, then You will set me firmly in place where evil cannot move me. I will be like a big, solid rock, stronger than anything the devil can destroy. Your love and power protect me. As my faith in You grows, Father, please allow me to help my friends to build up their faith in You too. Amen.

EVENING

## Children Praise Him

*Through the praise of children and infants you have established a stronghold against your enemies, to silence the foe and the avenger.*

PSALM 8:2 NIV

Dear God, You love kids. When we call on You, You don't see us as little and weak. You pay just as much attention to our prayers as You do grown-ups' prayers. And when we put our faith in You, You can help us to do great things. Kids can lead others to You and serve You just as well as adults. So, God, I praise You! Show me how I can serve You. Amen.

MORNING

## In My Heart

*No one has seen God at any time. If we love one another, God abides in us, and His love has been perfected in us.*

1 JOHN 4:12 NKJV

Father, I can't see You with my eyes, but I see You in my heart. When I show someone loving-kindness or forgiveness, it's because You are in me and working through me. When I help or comfort someone, that's You working through me. When You help me in times of trouble and give me courage and strength, that's You too. I don't have to see with my eyes to know You're real. My heart says it's so.

EVENING

## I'm a Disciple

*To the Jews who had believed him, Jesus said, "If you hold to my teaching, you are really my disciples. Then you will know the truth, and the truth will set you free."*

JOHN 8:31–32 NIV

Jesus, those who follow Your teaching are Your disciples. I'm doing my best to learn from You, so I guess that makes me a disciple too! When I read about You in the Bible, I pay close attention to Your words. I trust that all Your teachings are true. The truth separates me from evil and keeps me doing what's right. Help me to be a good disciple, Jesus. Teach me even more about You.

MORNING

## No Falling!

*He will not let your feet go out from under you.*
*He Who watches over you will not sleep.*

PSALM 121:3 NLV

Dear God, my youth group went ice-skating last night. I'm sure You saw me slipping and sliding around out there. It was my first time, but I managed, with help from my friend, to stay on my feet. This morning's verse reminds me of that. When I face a challenge and worry about falling, You are the one who keeps me on my feet. You are always watching over me. Thanks for the reminder, God.

EVENING

## Change Me, Lord

*Yet you, LORD, are our Father. We are the clay,*
*you are the potter; we are all the work of your hand.*

ISAIAH 64:8 NIV

Heavenly Father, You are like a sculptor. We are like clay in Your hands. You created us knowing that You would be changing us, little by little, as we grow and move through our lives. I feel You changing me, God. You are making me stronger, braver, more understanding, and more forgiving. I am Your work in progress, and You will keep working on me until I get to heaven someday. Amen.

MORNING

## The Real Me

*I have chosen the way of truth.*

Psalm 119:30 NKJV

God, I'm afraid to be real with others. I worry they might not like me. Sometimes I'm not even real with You because I don't want You to know how much of a sinner I am. God, You want us to be our real selves. I have nothing to hide, so give me courage to put myself out there and show others the real me. Amen.

EVENING

## Wisdom, Knowledge, and Joy

*For God giveth to a man that is good in his sight wisdom, and knowledge, and joy.*

Ecclesiastes 2:26 KJV

Father God, tonight's Bible verse says there are rewards for my goodness. When I behave in ways that please You, You will reward me with wisdom, knowledge, and joy. Those things are special blessings. I want to be wise about decisions I make. I want to learn more about You. And I love it when You pour joy into my life. Thank You, God, for these rewards and all Your many blessings.

MORNING

## Cobwebs in My Soul

*"You will keep him in perfect peace,*
*whose mind is stayed on You."*
Isaiah 26:3 NKJV

Lord, I feel good when everything is in order. When my room is clean and my homework and chores are done, my heart feels light. I feel at peace and ready to relax. When I put off doing stuff, it's like cobwebs begin forming in my heart. When things are done, all the messiness is gone, and I have more time to concentrate on other things, especially my friendship with You. Amen.

EVENING

## Moving Past My Mistakes

*"The thief comes only to steal and kill and destroy;*
*I have come that they may have life, and have it to the full."*
John 10:10 NIV

Dear God, I tend to think about my past mistakes; and when I do that, a little voice in my heart says, "Shame on you," or "You're not good enough." It's not Your voice. It's the voice of evil trying to steal my peace. You've forgiven me for past mistakes. You have washed them away and want me to move forward. Help me to do that. Your voice is the only one I want to hear.

MORNING

## Lead Me, Lord

*O Lord, lead me in what is right and good, because of the ones who hate me. Make Your way straight in front of me.*

Psalm 5:8 NLV

God, You know how hard it is sometimes for me to know which way I should go. Tonight I ask that You be my guide. Please show me clearly the way You want me to follow. While I might question why we're going a certain way, You know what's best, and You have great plans for me. Keep my path straight, Lord. Don't allow anyone to lead me in the wrong direction.

EVENING

## Lift Me Up, God

*My eyes are ever on the Lord, for only he will release my feet from the snare.*

Psalm 25:15 NIV

Father, sometimes I get stuck making the same mistakes over and over—stuck in murky, muddy sin. There's only one way out. I have to look to You and keep my eyes on You. Sin can't hold me down then. With Your strong and mighty arms, You will lift me up and out of it. My eyes are set on You, God. Pick me up and set my feet on clean, solid ground.

MORNING

## Always at My Side

*The LORD will be at your side and will keep your foot from being snared.*

PROVERBS 3:26 NIV

Jesus, I praise You for always being by my side. As I go about my day and get busy, I often forget that You are there. Please forgive me for that. Not only are You by my side, You are also helping me through the day, keeping me on the right path doing what's pleasing to You. Thank You for always being with me and for being the best friend I will ever have.

EVENING

## A Friend Like Jesus

*One who loves purity of heart and whose speech is gracious, the king is his friend.*

PROVERBS 22:11 NASB

Dear Lord Jesus, You delight when I do the right things and try my hardest to please You. When I keep my heart clean of sin and when the words from my mouth are kind, gentle, and caring, I make You happy. The Bible says You are the King of all kings. How blessed I am that the King of heaven and earth is not only my Lord and Savior but also my friend!

MORNING

## Those Who Are Against Me

*Teach me Your way, O Lord. Lead me in a straight path, because of those who fight against me.*

PSALM 27:11 NLV

Heavenly Father, people can be so mean sometimes. There's a boy in my class who is mean to everyone. I don't think he has many friends. Yesterday he said mean things to me. You've taught me, Lord, to love my enemies and pray for them. When I do that, I know I'm following the straight path You've set for me. Will You help that boy, please? I want him to be happy and have friends.

EVENING

## Hope and a Future

*"For I know the plans I have for you," declares the LORD, "plans to prosper you and not to harm you, plans to give you hope and a future."*

JEREMIAH 29:11 NIV

Father, I can't know all the plans You have for me. You reveal them little by little. Most of the time, I don't understand how You are working Your plan for me. But then I look back and see You putting together the pieces of my life. I'll remember something that happened and say, "I get it! That was part of God's plan. If that hadn't happened, I wouldn't be where I am now."

DAY 242

MORNING

## A Divided Heart

*Teach me thy way, O LORD; I will walk in thy truth: unite my heart to fear thy name.*

PSALM 86:11 KJV

Lord God, I'm guilty of having a divided heart. Forgive me. I want to do Your will and please You, but I also want to do what I want. A divided heart is never at peace. When my heart is going in two different directions, please fix it. Help me to let go of my wants and to focus on You—Your way, Your truth, Your will, Your path. Amen.

EVENING

## Trust in the Savior

*Give your burdens to the LORD, and he will take care of you. He will not permit the godly to slip and fall.*

PSALM 55:22 NLT

Dear Lord Jesus, I trust You. When I give my problems and concerns to You, I know You will take care of them and work everything out for Your honor. You are always looking out for me. Remind me of that on days when I feel worried and alone. You are the one who saves me from trouble. You are Jesus, the one who loves me. Amen.

MORNING

## Beautiful in His Time

*He hath made every thing beautiful in his time.*

ECCLESIASTES 3:11 KJV

Father, I'm not good at waiting, and I don't always look at the bright side. When things don't go my way, I get discouraged. When I'm discouraged, everything around me looks ugly. Nothing seems right. Your Word says that You make everything beautiful in Your time. *Your* time, God. Not my time. I need to remember that. You turn things around. You make darkness turn to light. Help me to wait patiently for You. Amen.

EVENING

## God's Watchful Care

*The LORD watches over the foreigner and sustains the fatherless and the widow, but he frustrates the ways of the wicked.*

PSALM 146:9 NIV

Kind heavenly Father, You watch over the weak, the sad, and those who feel left out. When life feels unfair, You are the one who brings comfort and hope. You don't care where someone comes from or whether they're rich or poor. In Your eyes, everyone in the world is equal; and when they call on You, You treat them with kindness. Thank You for keeping all of us under Your watchful care. Amen.

DAY 244

MORNING

## Friends for Every Need

*A time to weep, and a time to laugh;*
*a time to mourn, and a time to dance.*
ECCLESIASTES 3:4 NKJV

Dear God, thank You for blessing me with an amazing group of friends. Each one brings a special gift to my friendship with them. Some make me laugh. Others are great at comforting me when I'm sad. I have friends who like to sing and dance with me, some who are good at teaching me new crafts, others who help with homework—all kinds of friends! I'm grateful for them, Lord. Amen.

EVENING

## I Promise

*"Therefore know that the LORD your God, He is God, the faithful God who keeps covenant and mercy for a thousand generations with those who love Him and keep His commandments."*
DEUTERONOMY 7:9 NKJV

Father, You never break a promise! I trust You to keep Your word forever. All You want from me is to love You and do my best to keep Your commandments. That's the hard part—keeping them. I know what pleases You, but I forget sometimes and go my own way. I'm not going to promise that I'll keep all Your commandments perfectly, because no human can do that. But I promise to do my best.

MORNING

## Morning Love

*Let me hear Your loving-kindness in the morning, for I trust in You. Teach me the way I should go for I lift up my soul to You.*

Psalm 143:8 NLV

God, I love talking with You first thing in the morning. If I take time to listen to Your voice in my heart, I will hear Your loving-kindness as You send me on my way. Lead me today. Help me to stay focused on You and the path You've set for me. Follow me into the evening and whisper loving thoughts to me at night as I rest my head, ready to meet You again.

EVENING

## Abundant Blessings

*God is able to bless you abundantly, so that in all things at all times, having all that you need, you will abound in every good work.*

2 Corinthians 9:8 NIV

Lord God, when my hands and heart do the right thing, it's because of You. Doing what's right leads to abundant blessings. Following the path You've set for me brings glory to Your kingdom. It is a way of bringing Your light into the world. Father, I want to share Your love with everyone I know. I want my family and friends to know and follow You, so they too will be blessed abundantly. Amen.

DAY 246

MORNING

## God Is Watching Me

*I will instruct thee and teach thee in the way which thou shalt go: I will guide thee with mine eye.*

PSALM 32:8 KJV

Dear God, I know You are always watching me. You want me to keep my eyes on You too. When I focus on what You might be trying to teach me, I know You will guide me on the right path. Thank You, Father, for watching over me. You see what's ahead of me. Open my eyes to follow You. I trust You, because You know the direction I should go. Amen.

EVENING

## Forever Goodness and Loving-Kindness

*For sure, You will give me goodness and loving-kindness all the days of my life. Then I will live with You in Your house forever.*

PSALM 23:6 NLV

Lord, Your goodness and loving-kindness are with me *every* day, not just on days when everything goes right. On days when I feel sad, lonely, discouraged, or afraid, You still help me to focus on Your kindness and goodness. Every day of my life, You are with me, loving and caring for me. One day I will meet You in heaven. Then I will thank You in person for all You have done for me.

MORNING

## Freedom to Share

*Be happy that you are able to share some of the suffering of Christ. When His shining-greatness is shown, you will be filled with much joy.*

1 Peter 4:13 NLV

Dear God, the Bible talks about Your followers Paul and Silas. They were put in prison for preaching about You. While in jail, they sang hymns to You and prayed. Other prisoners heard and learned what it means to serve and love You. Remind me, Lord, to share You with others. I'm free to speak about You. Let me use the gift of my freedom to serve You. Amen.

EVENING

## God Beside Me

*You are near, O Lord, and all your commands are true.*

Psalm 119:151 NLT

Thank You, Lord, for being at my side, especially when trouble gets in my way. Thank You for the double promise in tonight's scripture verse: You will always stay by me and will never change Your commands. I praise You, God. No one stands by me like You. There's nothing You won't do for me. Every day, help me to keep my eyes on You and do my best to follow Your commands. Amen.

MORNING

## Moving and Making Friends

*A man who has friends must himself be friendly.*

PROVERBS 18:24 NKJV

Dear heavenly Father, my family moves a lot. I don't like moving, because I have to leave my friends behind and make new friends. I feel like crying because today is the first day at a new school. I need Your help. It's time to go to school, smile, introduce myself, and be friendly. Lord, help me to make new friends today. Help me to be brave. Here we go. . .

EVENING

## Before I Was Born

*Your eyes saw my substance, being yet unformed.*
*And in Your book they all were written, the days fashioned*
*for me, when as yet there were none of them.*

PSALM 139:16 NKJV

Father, even before I was born, You had planned every day of my life. You had Your plan for me all written down in Your book. I can't even imagine that! You put me on earth exactly when You wanted and for some special purpose. The days ahead of me are a mystery, but You already have them in Your control. Let me honor You, Father, and serve You all the days of my life.

MORNING

# For My Own Good

*The Lord Who bought you and saves you, the Holy One of Israel, says, "I am the Lord your God, Who teaches you to do well, Who leads you in the way you should go."*

ISAIAH 48:17 NLV

Sometimes I forget, Lord, that Your guidance is always for my own good. Some of Your lessons are hard; but still, it's important that I learn them. You want what's best for me. If I follow You and Your teaching, You will lead me to peace, joy, and blessings. Guide me to trust You more today and every day. Thank You, Lord. Amen.

EVENING

# Anger

*Get rid of all bitterness, rage and anger, brawling and slander, along with every form of malice.*

EPHESIANS 4:31 NIV

God, You know what happened. I need to let go of this angry feeling and give it to You. Help me get rid of it. I need to calm down and feel Your loving-kindness. Help me let go of feeling I want to get even. Show me if I had any part in what went wrong today. Forgive me, and help me to forgive the person who hurt me. Please bring me healing and peace.

MORNING

## Voices in My Heart

*Your ears will hear a word behind you, saying, "This is the way, walk in it," whenever you turn to the right or to the left.*

ISAIAH 30:21 NLV

Dear Father, I want to get better at knowing Your voice in my heart. Your voice begins in my heart, and then I hear it in my head. Your voice tells me the difference between right and wrong and guides me on the right path. Other voices speak to my heart. They tell me to do what goes against Your will. Help me to know the difference and to obey only You.

EVENING

## Sadness Won't Last Forever

*Weeping may last through the night,*
*but joy comes with the morning.*

PSALM 30:5 NLT

Lord, I feel sad tonight. It feels like I'll be sad forever. Joy seems far away. But You remind me that the sadness will go away. I have hope that tomorrow will be a better day. You already know what tomorrow holds, and I trust You to bring some happiness into my day. Tonight, God, comfort me. Watch over me and give me rest. I look forward to starting fresh in the morning.

MORNING

# Nothing but the Truth

*"Then you will know the truth,*
*and the truth will set you free."*
JOHN 8:32 NIV

Dear God, from the very beginning, humans were tricked by evil. The devil whispered to Eve to go against Your command, and she listened. Ever since, humans have been listening to his lies. Help me to be careful not to fall for Satan's evil ways. Make me wise, Lord. Set me free from the devil's words. I want to know Your will and follow it as the only absolute truth.

EVENING

# When My Faith Is Weak

*"Blessed is the one who trusts in the LORD,*
*whose confidence is in him."*
JEREMIAH 17:7 NIV

God, my trust lies in You. You control everything in heaven and on earth. My problems seem big to me; but to You, my situation looks simple and small. Nothing I face surprises You. Thank You for giving me tonight's verse to hold on to when my faith is weak. Though I may not see it yet, You are blessing me. Help me continue to trust You as You lead me from day to day.

## DAY 252

### MORNING

# Happy in the Lord

*The LORD's delight is in those who fear him,*
*those who put their hope in his unfailing love.*
PSALM 147:11 NLT

You delight in me, Lord—that means I make You happy! In Your delight, You shower me with blessings and Your love. I feel in my heart that You are pleased with me for making right decisions. I want to honor You and bring You joy every day. Keep me focused on Your faithfulness to me so I can be faithful to You too. I love You, Lord. You make me happy. Amen.

### EVENING

# Come Together in Love

*Be kind to each other, tenderhearted, forgiving one*
*another, just as God through Christ has forgiven you.*
EPHESIANS 4:32 NLT

Dear God, I can't believe that my best friend and I argued over such a silly thing. I didn't think it was a big deal, but she did. I'm still hurt over what she said. Maybe she feels the same about what I said. Please help us both to forgive each other and come back together as friends. I love my friend, God. Help me to show her nothing but kindness and understanding. Amen.

MORNING

## Open Their Eyes

*"I will lead the blind by a way that they do not know. I will lead them in paths they do not know. I will turn darkness into light in front of them. And I will make the bad places smooth. These are the things I will do and I will not leave them."*

ISAIAH 42:16 NLV

Father, when people don't know You, it's almost as if they are blind. But when You come into their hearts, You open their eyes. You show them Your mighty power and light up their lives with Your love. If they choose to follow You, then You lead them down a path toward goodness. You promise never to leave them or let them down. Lord, I want others to know You. Please open their eyes. Amen.

EVENING

## Slow to Anger

*The LORD is gracious and full of compassion, slow to anger and great in mercy.*

PSALM 145:8 NKJV

God, if I were You, I'd be angry when I see all the bad stuff going on in the world. But the Bible says You are slow to get angry. To those who love You, You are forever kind, forgiving, and caring. In Your own time and way, You will deal with the world's sin. Will You help me to be more patient and slower to anger? I want to become more like You. Amen.

MORNING

## Jesus' Mother

*"For He who is mighty has done great things for me, and holy is His name."*
LUKE 1:49 NKJV

Dear Father God, thank You for the example set by Mary, Jesus' mother. I thank You for her example of selflessness and praise. She brought honor to You. She helped You raise Your Son and then witnessed His death and resurrection. You took an ordinary girl and made her the most extraordinary mom of all time. What an amazing purpose You had for her life. Amen.

EVENING

## To Understand the Bible

*You made me and formed me with your hands. Give me understanding so I can learn your commands.*
PSALM 119:73 NCV

Lord God, the Bible is Your Word for my life. Help me to understand what You are saying to me. Give me wisdom as I read the scripture verses You guide me to every day. I know that if I read and think about Your words, I will grow and learn more about You. Throughout every day, bring the words I've read into my mind, and help me to apply them to everything I do.

MORNING

# The Path of Life

*You will show me the way of life. Being with You is to be full of joy. In Your right hand there is happiness forever.*

PSALM 16:11 NLV

Why do I run on ahead of You, Lord? Sometimes my way seems better, so I take a side trip off the path You've made for me. When I do that, I get lost. My path leads to disappointment, anger, and even shame. I know Your path leads to Your loving-kindness. Along the way, I'll find goodness that lasts forever. Help me, Father, to keep walking straight ahead on Your path and not my own.

EVENING

# Loving...

*"The Lord, the Lord God, with loving-pity and loving-favor, slow to anger, filled with loving-kindness and truth."*

EXODUS 34:6 NLV

God, You fill my heart with Your love. When I ask You to bless me, You fill me up with Your loving favor. When I mess up, You are slow to anger and quick to forgive. If I need help deciding, You guide me toward the truth and help me make the right choice. If I'm sad, Your loving pity comforts me. You show me Your loving-kindness, Lord, in so many ways, and I thank You. Amen.

DAY 256

MORNING

# Forgive and Forgive Again

*"Forgive, and you will be forgiven."*

LUKE 6:37 NIV

Dear Lord, You and I have this "forgiving" conversation a lot. Your Word says You want me to forgive people who hurt me. I want to forgive them, but the actual forgiving part is really hard. I still feel angry in my heart, and I need to let that go. So, Father, here is my anger. Take it, and please replace it with forgiveness in my heart. Amen.

EVENING

# Lasting Love

*Give thanks to the God of gods.*
*His faithful love endures forever.*

PSALM 136:2 NLT

Dear God, nothing can stop You from loving me. Your love will last forever, because no one and nothing is greater than You. If You seem far away sometimes, help me still to believe and trust in Your love. I'm so grateful that You—God of the universe—love me! I want to show You my love in return by following Your commands and serving You. I love You, Father. Amen.

MORNING

## Standing Up Straight

*Teach me to do thy will; for thou art my God:*
*thy spirit is good; lead me into the land of uprightness.*
PSALM 143:10 KJV

Jesus, everything that's been going on lately is pressing down on me. It's like I have the biggest and heaviest backpack ever slung over my shoulders! I feel tired, and I'm done carrying all this weight. Jesus, You remind me that You are strong enough to carry the weight of the world. So I give You my troubles. Take that weight off me, and help me to stand up refreshed, straight, and tall.

EVENING

## Glad Life

*Those without pride will see it and be glad.*
*You who look for God, let your heart receive new strength.*
PSALM 69:32 NLV

When I think that I can handle my problems all by myself, God, You find ways to remind me that I need You. Strength in challenging situations doesn't come from me alone. It comes from You. When I look for You, talk with You, and ask for Your help, You readily give it. You are the one who makes me strong. When I feel Your strength pouring into my heart, I feel glad.

DAY 258

## MORNING

# Older Women

*Older women are to teach the young women to love their husbands and children.*

TITUS 2:4 NLV

I wonder, God, if I will be a wife and mom when I grow up. When I get older and go on dates, remind me to talk to my mom and other older women about my concerns. Please give them the words to give me good advice. Open my eyes to older women who are good role models for my future. Guide me to make good choices as I move closer to being a grown-up.

## EVENING

# Eternal Life

*"As Moses lifted up the serpent in the wilderness, even so must the Son of Man be lifted up, that whoever believes in Him should not perish but have eternal life."*

JOHN 3:14–15 NKJV

Dear God, our goal since the beginning of time is forever life in heaven with You. Before You sent Jesus, people didn't have the promise of eternal life. But because You loved us, You sent Your Son and made it possible just by believing in Him to live with You in heaven when we die. I'm grateful, God, for Your gift of heaven. Thank You for sending us Jesus! Amen.

MORNING

## Search My Heart

*See if there be any wicked way in me,*
*and lead me in the way everlasting.*
PSALM 139:24 KJV

Father, search my heart; and if You find anything in there that You don't like, show me and help me get rid of it. Sometimes I'm not even aware of the sin that's inside me. It hides in there and then comes out when I have to decide between right and wrong. I want the goodness in my heart to be everlasting—to go on forever. Guide me away from sin and toward You. Amen.

EVENING

## Lord, Give Me Patience

*Better is the end of a thing than the beginning of it,*
*and the patient in spirit is better than the proud in spirit.*
ECCLESIASTES 7:8 AMPC

Lord, going my own way lands me in trouble. But patiently waiting for You and following Your commands lead to good things. I have to admit that I'm not very patient, especially when I'm in a hurry. I want things now, and I want people to do things my way. Lead me away from selfishness. I want You to control my life. Whatever I do today, Lord, give me patience.

MORNING

## Negative Feelings, Positive Prayers

*"Love your enemies and pray for those who persecute you, that you may be children of your Father in heaven."*

MATTHEW 5:44–45 NIV

Lord God, thank You for this morning's Bible verse. It tells me that praying for those who hurt me is a positive thing. I can't hold on to negative feelings about others when I'm lifting them up to You in prayer. Today's verse is very clear that You expect me, Your child, to have a heart that forgives and loves at all times. Thank You for the reminder, Lord. Amen.

EVENING

## In Control

*The LORD's plans stand firm forever; his intentions can never be shaken.*

PSALM 33:11 NLT

Whether it's something as small as a molecule or atom or something huge like the universe, it belongs to You, God. You created everything with a perfect plan. You know from beginning to end exactly how things will work out, and nothing can change that. Your plans are solid and firm. I'm glad about that because I know whatever happens, I don't have to worry. You have it all in Your control.

MORNING

## The Same Old Me

*You have searched me, LORD, and you know me.*

PSALM 139:1 NIV

Jesus, my self-esteem is sinking. Will You help me love myself just as I am? That's how You love me! Help me see myself through Your eyes. Remind me that I'm Your work in progress. I want to grow to be more like You in everything I say and do. Each day You are teaching me to become better. Help me focus on the good things about me, not what I think are my flaws.

EVENING

## Be Still and Rest

*"Be still, and know that I am God; I will be exalted among the nations, I will be exalted in the earth."*

PSALM 46:10 NIV

Dear Lord, I'm a girl who is always on the move. I keep busy. School takes up most of my day; activities take up the rest. By bedtime, I'm so tired I just want to sleep. But sometimes my mind keeps racing. Please, when I lie down at night, help me to be still and keep my thoughts set on You. Give me a good night's rest so I will be ready for tomorrow. Amen.

DAY 262

MORNING

# It's Not So Bad

*I am sure that our suffering now cannot be compared to the shining-greatness that He is going to give us.*

ROMANS 8:18 NLV

Heavenly Father, please forgive me when I complain. I have good reasons sometimes to wish things were going better for me, but nothing compares to the suffering Jesus went through. He suffered in my place so I'd be able to live with You one day in heaven. When things aren't going my way, will You please help me to remember Jesus and have the best attitude I can? Thank You. Amen.

EVENING

# Peace with Others

*Live in peace with each other.*

1 THESSALONIANS 5:13 NIV

Lord, some people are hard to be around. A boy in my class thinks he's funny, but he's not. There's a girl who talks too much and wants attention. I'm sure there are things about me that irritate others too. Different personalities don't always fit together; still, You want us to live in peace. I want to be okay with people just as they are. Will You help with that, please?

MORNING

## Little Troubles

*The little troubles we suffer now for a short time are making us ready for the great things God is going to give us forever.*

2 CORINTHIANS 4:17 NLV

God, I've learned an important lesson: Little troubles make me strong. When I rely on You to lead me through the little troubles, I grow my faith and trust in You. I also grow in wisdom. I can take what I've learned with little troubles and apply them to bigger problems in my life. With You at my side forever, there will be no trouble too big for You and me to handle together.

EVENING

## Contentment

*A God-like life gives us much when we are happy for what we have.*

1 TIMOTHY 6:6 NLV

Father, when I think about Jesus, He didn't have a lot of stuff. Yet He had everything because He had You! Contentment—being happy and satisfied—doesn't come from having a bunch of things. It comes from You living in my heart. When I think of You as my everything, then whatever else I have is a blessing. And I have so many blessings, Lord. Thanks to You and Your loving-kindness, I am content.

DAY 264

MORNING

# Patient and Loving

*You are from God, little children, and have overcome them; because greater is He who is in you than he who is in the world.*

1 JOHN 4:4 NASB

Dear God, I'm slow at learning Your lessons, but You are patient and loving. Thank You for not giving up on me as I learn. You are willing to go at my pace, forgiving me when I fail and picking me up with confidence to try again. Each day You give me a fresh start, and I feel joy flood my heart that You, my teacher, are there to guide me.

EVENING

# Thanks for My Mom

*She watches over the affairs of her household and does not eat the bread of idleness.*

PROVERBS 31:27 NIV

Dear God, thank You for my mom. I appreciate all she does for us. She is the first one up in the morning to help my siblings and me get ready for school. She works hard at her job and keeps everything running smoothly at home. She always makes time for us even when she's busy. I love her, God. Remind me to tell her every day about how much she means to me. Amen.

MORNING

# A Better Plan

*There are many plans in a man's heart,*
*but it is the Lord's plan that will stand.*

PROVERBS 19:21 NLV

Father God, I get frustrated when I have a project under control and then something happens to mess it up. I'd just finished writing an essay when my tablet crashed. I lost everything and had to do it over. It was a blessing in disguise, though, because when I rewrote my essay, it turned out great. Your Word says Your plan will stand. My plan was good, but Yours was even better. Thanks, God! Amen.

EVENING

# Beautiful!

*I praise you because I am fearfully*
*and wonderfully made.*

PSALM 139:14 NIV

Dear heavenly Father, when I shop for clothes, I want to look like the older teen models I see. But I never end up looking like them, and then I feel depressed. I know that isn't what You want for me. Help me with these feelings, and show me that I'm beautiful inside and outside just the way You made me. Amen.

DAY 266

MORNING

## Jesus Gives Me Hope

*Looking for that blessed hope, and the glorious appearing of the great God and our Saviour Jesus Christ.*

Titus 2:13 KJV

Father, I have many hopes and dreams. Sometimes I feel I'm getting close to making some come true. Other times my dreams feel far away, and I cling to a single thread of hope. On those days, remind me to put all my hope in Jesus. He's the one I need to help me form hopes and dreams that line up with Your will, and He will guide me to make those dreams come true.

EVENING

## A Family Praying Together

*He and all his family were devout and God-fearing; he gave generously to those in need and prayed to God regularly.*

Acts 10:2 NIV

Dear Father God, I want my family to pray together more often. When we pray before meals and have other times of prayer together, we are putting You first. Praying together honors You as we thank You for each other and the many ways You bless us. When our family prays together, it brings us nearer not only to You but also to each other. Bring us together in prayer, Lord. Amen.

MORNING

## Meeting Jesus

*When Christ, who is our life, shall appear,*
*then shall ye also appear with him in glory.*

COLOSSIANS 3:4 KJV

Jesus, when I read about You in the Bible, I imagine what You looked like and what Your voice sounded like. I have a picture of You in my mind. One day I'll meet You face-to-face, and then I will know what You look like. I think I will recognize You because I know You so well. You live inside my heart. You are with me every day, and You will be with me forever.

EVENING

## I Choose You, Lord

*"But if serving the LORD seems undesirable to you,*
*then choose for yourselves this day whom you will serve. . . .*
*But as for me and my household, we will serve the LORD."*

JOSHUA 24:15 NIV

Dear Lord, You allow us to make our own choices. It's been that way since the beginning, when Eve had a choice to obey You or follow Satan and eat from the forbidden tree. I want to make the right choices. I want to serve You in all that I do. Father, I choose to follow You. Guide me in the right direction. Lead me to make choices that are in line with Your will.

MORNING

# The Power of Words

*Death and life are in the power of the tongue:*
*and they that love it shall eat the fruit thereof.*

PROVERBS 18:21 KJV

Father, words are powerful. Words can hurt so badly they make people cry. Words can be so loving they bring tears of joy. Words can give poor advice or advice that's wise. Remind me that it's important to choose my words wisely and to be wise when listening to the words of others. Your words in the Bible are the most powerful of all. I'll do my best to live by them every day. Amen.

EVENING

# A New Mind

*Do not act like the sinful people of the world. Let God change your life. First of all, let Him give you a new mind. Then you will know what God wants you to do. And the things you do will be good and pleasing and perfect.*

ROMANS 12:2 NLV

Heavenly Father, my emotions need a makeover. I ask for Your power to change. Help me to let go of feeling angry and disappointed when things don't go my way. Clear my mind of any selfish and unhealthy thoughts. Guide me to know what You want me to do. Then help me to follow Your will so that whatever I do will be pleasing and perfect in Your sight. Amen.

MORNING

## God's Thoughts

*For I know the thoughts that I think toward you, saith the LORD, thoughts of peace, and not of evil, to give you an expected end.*

JEREMIAH 29:11 KJV

Dear God, You know how easily my thoughts turn to worries and fears. Teach me to think Your thoughts. Give me wise thoughts and thoughts of peace and goodness that will lead to the future You have planned for me. Show me the steps I need to take as I grow to become an adult. Keep my thoughts centered on You with each step I take. My faith and trust are in You. Amen.

EVENING

## Changing My Thoughts

*May the words of my mouth and the meditation of my heart be pleasing to you, O LORD, my rock and my redeemer.*

PSALM 19:14 NLT

Heavenly Father, Your Word says I can choose what to think about and what I say. I want my thoughts and my words to be pleasing to You. Help me to choose wisely. Keep my mind set on the Bible verses I have learned. Help me to apply them to all that I say and do. When my mind wanders away from You and Your Word, please lead me back. Amen.

DAY 270

MORNING

## God Chose Me

*"You did not choose me, but I chose you and appointed you so that you might go and bear fruit—fruit that will last."*

John 15:16 NIV

I often forget, Lord, that I didn't choose You—You chose me. You chose to create me and give me life. You chose me for this specific time on earth. You allow me the choice of following You and Your Word or not. Father, I choose to follow You. Show me how to serve You. How can I use the skills and talents You've given me to do Your work here on earth? Amen.

EVENING

## Jesus Rescues Me

*"Because he loves me," says the Lord, "I will rescue him; I will protect him, for he acknowledges my name."*

Psalm 91:14 NIV

"I will rescue him; I will protect him." Jesus, what a great promise in tonight's Bible verse! I've seen it happen. When I've needed help with something, You've sent the kind of help I've needed even before I asked for it. Whether it was someone to help with my homework or someone to save me from getting hurt, You were there to rescue me. Thank You, Jesus, for loving me and watching over me. Amen.

MORNING

## God Cannot Lie

*This truth also gives hope of life that lasts forever. God promised this before the world began. He cannot lie.*

Titus 1:2 NLV

God, the Bible doesn't say that You *will not* lie; it says You *cannot* lie. Lying is a sin, and there's no sin at all in You. Every word You say in the Bible is perfectly true. I can count on that. All Your promises are forever. Because Your words are true, they give us hope for the future. Whatever You say will come true in Your own time and in the ways You've planned.

EVENING

## How Great Is God?

*Great is the Lord and most worthy of praise;*
*his greatness no one can fathom.*

Psalm 145:3 NIV

Father God, people say, "God is great!" But no one can imagine the total power of Your greatness. We humans look at things through earthly eyes. What You've done on earth, we see as great and magnificent. But it's just a small glimpse of Your greatness. So much of who You are is unseen. Someday when we get to heaven, we will see with heavenly eyes how great You really are. Amen.

MORNING

# I Don't Understand

*Oh, the depth of the riches, both of the wisdom and knowledge of God! How unsearchable are His judgments and unfathomable His ways!*

ROMANS 11:33 NASB

God, when I start to feel as though You may not know what You're doing, remind me that Your wisdom and knowledge are far greater than mine. When I don't understand why You've done something, help me to put my faith in You, knowing that Your ways are always perfect and part of a plan that I cannot see. Give me peace when I don't understand. Amen.

EVENING

# Fruit of the Spirit

*The fruit that comes from having the Holy Spirit in our lives is: love, joy, peace, not giving up, being kind, being good, having faith, being gentle, and being the boss over our own desires. The Law is not against these things.*

GALATIANS 5:22–23 NLV

Dear Lord, tonight's verse is a reminder of all the good "fruit" that comes into our hearts when we follow You. You've been helping me become better at goodness and also at showing kindness and gentleness to others. You've been building up my faith in You. I could use more help, though, with the part about being the boss over my own desires. Continue to teach me, God. I'm willing. Amen.

MORNING

## Let There Be Light!

*Then God said, "Let there be light"; and there was light. God saw that the light was good; and God separated the light from the darkness.*

GENESIS 1:3–4 NASB

I like being creative, God. I'm good at painting and drawing. Every project I do takes time. I think about colors I want to use and whether I'll create with paint or crayons. But You, God? All You need to do when You create something is speak it into existence. How much fun that must be! Maybe when I get to heaven, You will let me speak a work of art into appearing before my very eyes.

EVENING

## New Friends

*If one falls down, the other can help him up. But it is bad for the person who is alone and falls, because no one is there to help.*

ECCLESIASTES 4:10 NCV

Dear God, my mom and dad are both in the military, and our family moves around a lot. It's hard leaving friends behind. I always feel lonely when I get someplace new. Give me the courage and strength to reach out and make new friends. I know You have some special friends waiting for me in the future—good friends that will last a lifetime. Help me find them, please. Thank You, God. Amen.

MORNING

## Just for a While

*After you have suffered for awhile, God Himself will make you perfect. He will keep you in the right way. He will give you strength. He is the God of all loving-favor and has called you through Christ Jesus to share His shining-greatness forever.*

1 PETER 5:10 NLV

Dear God, I often wish You would act sooner. When I face trouble or a challenge, I want You to sweep right in and fix it. But usually You don't. You know that it's through trouble that I learn more about You. I learn to trust You no matter what. I've learned that, in Your own timing, You will fix things according to Your will. Amen.

EVENING

## Giving God Control of My Future

*People may make plans in their minds,*
*but the LORD decides what they will do.*

PROVERBS 16:9 NCV

Jesus, You knew that God's will was for You to give Your life so that others may know God and go to heaven after they die. You gave God total control and submitted to His will. Help me do the same. You have a plan for my life, and I want to complete everything You created me to accomplish. You are in control. Help me to live my life according to Your perfect plan.

MORNING

## Above All I Think or Ask

*[God] is able to do exceeding abundantly above all that we ask or think, according to the power that worketh in us.*

EPHESIANS 3:20 KJV

Father, I put limits on what I think I can accomplish. That's not good! With Your help, I know I can accomplish even more. Give me courage to try. If something is outside my comfort zone, help me to take that first step. Give me wisdom with each step I take so that I'm always in step with You. Help me to expect great things in my future when You and I work together.

EVENING

## Security Guard

*He guards the paths of the just and protects those who are faithful to him.*

PROVERBS 2:8 NLT

Father, when I walk that imaginary path into my future, I imagine You guarding me all along the way. I know You will protect me because I've been faithful to You. You keep Your eyes focused ahead. You know what obstacles might get in my way, and You have a plan to keep me safe. Thank You for guarding me today and all the days of my life. Amen.

DAY 276

MORNING

## My Shelter

*"The Lord lives. Thanks be to my Rock.*
*May God be honored, the Rock that saves me."*
2 SAMUEL 22:47 NLV

Father, I live where there are lots of storms. If there's a storm warning, we have a shelter we go to. It's made of strong concrete blocks. When we're inside, we know we'll be safe. You are like a shelter in a storm. I can run to You and feel safe inside Your love. Your strength protects me. Nothing can harm me when I am with You. You are the "rock" that saves me. Amen.

EVENING

## True Love

*Above all, love each other deeply,*
*because love covers over a multitude of sins.*
1 PETER 4:8 NIV

True love is when You love someone even when they mess up. Jesus, You love me when I disappoint You. My parents don't stop loving me when I disappoint them either. Tonight's Bible verse reminds me that true love means forgiving. I want to love with that kind of love. If someone hurts me, I want to be able to forgive their sin and keep right on loving them. Please help me do that. Amen.

MORNING

## No Spirit of Fear

*For God hath not given us the spirit of fear;*
*but of power, and of love, and of a sound mind.*
2 TIMOTHY 1:7 KJV

Dear God, there are things I'm afraid of. They aren't big things, but they're embarrassing because I think most kids don't have the same fear. I haven't told anyone except You what I'm afraid of. I ask You to help me. It's normal to feel afraid sometimes. Help me not to worry about sharing my fears with my parents and other people I trust. And please help me, God, not to be so afraid. Amen.

EVENING

## It's Important to Save

*The wise store up choice food and olive oil,*
*but fools gulp theirs down.*
PROVERBS 21:20 NIV

Heavenly Father, I'm not so good at saving. When I get some money, I'm already thinking about how I can spend it. When I get a food treat, I'm ready to gobble it all up. I know saving is important. It teaches patience. It's good to put some of what I have aside for later when I might want or need it. I'm going to try harder to save. Will You help me? Amen.

MORNING

# God Lights My Path

*The path of the just is as the shining light, that shineth more and more unto the perfect day.*

PROVERBS 4:18 KJV

Father, when I put all my faith in You and give You control of my life, the path You've made for me seems clearer. It's as if You are shining a light into the future. You ask me to follow You; and with each correct step I take, Your light shines even brighter. Keep leading me on the right path, God. I feel good about the direction I'm going right now. Amen.

EVENING

# Jesus Lives in My Heart

*We are the temple of the living God. As God has said: "I will live with them and walk among them, and I will be their God, and they will be my people."*

2 CORINTHIANS 6:16 NIV

Jesus, when I asked You to come into my heart, You didn't come for a visit; You came to live inside me. Your Spirit is with me all the time. I feel You showing me the way I should go, leading and guiding me. I hear Your voice speaking to my heart; I feel You making me strong and keeping me safe. Thank You for being my God and wanting to live with me forever.

MORNING

## Pack for the Future

*Now faith is the certainty of things hoped for, a proof of things not seen.*
HEBREWS 11:1 NASB

Lord, I wonder what my future holds. Your world is so beautiful and so large. I want to see it all, but I know that isn't possible. I'm sure, though, that in my lifetime You will allow me to see plenty of what I want to see here on earth. You've already opened my eyes to some very cool things! I praise You for what is and for what will be. Amen.

EVENING

## The Message Is for Everyone!

*God wants these great riches of the hidden truth to be made known to the people who are not Jews. The secret is this: Christ in you brings hope of all the great things to come.*
COLOSSIANS 1:27 NLV

Dear God, the Old Testament is about Your relationship with the Jews. They were Your chosen people. But when Jesus came, He told His followers, "You are to go to all the world and preach the Good News to every person" (Mark 16:15 NLV). The good news that Jesus has forgiven our sins and is our way to heaven is a message for everyone. Help me to share it wherever I go. Amen.

MORNING

## Feeling Sorry for Myself

*Fix your thoughts on what is true, and honorable, and right, and pure, and lovely, and admirable.*

PHILIPPIANS 4:8 NLT

Dear God, I woke up this morning feeling sorry for myself. It's one of those days when I'd rather stay in bed than go to school. My thoughts are so focused on myself that I'm having trouble focusing on You. Please forgive me. You can't work through me when I'm feeling sorry for myself. Help me to focus on good, praiseworthy things. Then lead me into this day with a happy, joyful heart. Amen.

EVENING

## Sadness

*Why, my soul, are you downcast? Why so disturbed within me? Put your hope in God, for I will yet praise him.*

PSALM 42:5 NIV

Lord, I had a bad day. I feel like crying myself to sleep. Help me to remember that even when I'm sad, I can choose to put my hope in You. Thinking about what happened today will only make me sadder. Remind me of the good things You've done in the past. I hope—I *know!*—You have good things waiting for me tomorrow. Tonight just comfort me and let me rest in Your love.

MORNING

## Like Jesus

*Dear friends, we are God's children now. But it has not yet been shown to us what we are going to be. We know that when He comes again, we will be like Him because we will see Him as He is.*

1 John 3:2 NLV

Dear Jesus, I'm Your work in progress. Each day You teach me to be a little more like You. Your teaching will go on all through my life. When I get to heaven someday, I wonder how I will change. The Bible says we can't know until we get there what we are going to be. Then we will see You as You are and be like You. Continue to teach me, Lord. Amen.

EVENING

## Stronghold

*The Lord is a refuge for the oppressed, a stronghold in times of trouble.*

Psalm 9:9 NIV

Dear God, I looked up *stronghold*. It means a place built with strong material to protect it against an attack. I imagine a fort or a castle with walls made of stone. The Bible says You are my "stronghold in times of trouble." Nothing can harm You, God. You are more powerful than anything! With You protecting me, I don't have to be afraid. Guard my heart. Protect me wherever I go. Amen.

MORNING

## Face-to-Face

*For now we see through a glass, darkly;*
*but then face to face: now I know in part;*
*but then shall I know even as also I am known.*
1 CORINTHIANS 13:12 KJV

Dear heavenly Father, You know that I can't see You clearly. You know I don't really understand You, even when I am seeking You every day and asking You for answers. I'm grateful, though, that I expect to see You face-to-face in heaven one day. On that day, I will finally know You completely. I hope You'll be ready for all my questions, God, because I have a ton of them!

EVENING

## Everyone Can Be Saved

*And so Jesus is able, now and forever, to save from*
*the punishment of sin all who come to God through*
*Him because He lives forever to pray for them.*
HEBREWS 7:25 NLV

Dear Jesus, I confess that I judge people sometimes. I read or hear about people who do really bad things, and I think those people will never get into heaven. But tonight's Bible verse says You are able to save *all* who come to You. So, instead of judging them, Lord, I need to pray for those people. I want everyone to come to You and be saved. Amen.

MORNING

## Fadeless Beauty

*The unfading beauty of a gentle and quiet spirit. . .is so precious to God.*

1 PETER 3:4 NLT

Dear God, some girls think beauty is everything. Their whole world is makeup and designer clothes. I like to look nice, but I know beauty on the inside is way more important than what a person looks like on the outside. When You look at me, the first thing You see is my heart. A quiet and gentle spirit will last forever while beauty on the outside fades away. Thanks for the reminder, God. Amen.

EVENING

## God's Child Forever

*Everyone who believes that Jesus is the Christ has become a child of God.*

1 JOHN 5:1 NLT

I get it, Father! Your children never grow old. Their bodies get old and die; but in their hearts, everyone who believes in Your Son, Jesus, will be Your child forever. You love and protect Your children from the day they are born until they die. You are always teaching them to become more like You. And when they move from earth to heaven, they will still be Your children and live with You forever.

# DAY 284

## MORNING

## Changed!

*All of us, with no covering on our faces, show the shining-greatness of the Lord as in a mirror. All the time we are being changed to look like Him, with more and more of His shining-greatness.*

2 Corinthians 3:18 NLV

God, how wonderful that You want to change me to look more like You! It's not about changing my body to look like Yours—it's about changing my spirit, my heart, to be more like Yours. Every time I follow Your commands and choose right over wrong, I'm changing to become more like You. Keep making those changes in me. Let Your Spirit shine through me like an image in a mirror. Amen.

## EVENING

## Sing with Gladness

*So the people, for whom the Lord paid the price to be saved, will return. They will come with songs of joy to Zion. Joy that lasts forever will be on their heads. They will receive joy and happiness, and sorrow and sad voices will hurry away.*

Isaiah 51:11 NLV

Jesus, heaven must be filled with joyful singing because everyone there is happy. I'm happy too, because You saved me from sin. Knowing that one day I'm going to be with You in heaven and join in the singing makes me glad. But for now, I'll sing to You from earth. When I sing praise songs, I know You'll hear them in heaven, and I think that brings You joy.

MORNING

## All Things New

*And He who sits on the throne said, "Behold, I am making all things new."*

REVELATION 21:5 NASB

Almighty God, Your Word says that someday the whole creation will be liberated from its bondage to decay and brought into glorious freedom. In fact, the whole creation groans, waiting to be made new (Romans 8:21–22). One day You will make this old earth go away. Death will be replaced with life, and Your masterpiece will be finished—and it will be perfect, just as You planned.

EVENING

## Pure

*Every word of God is pure; He is a shield to those who put their trust in Him.*

PROVERBS 30:5 NKJV

Father, tonight's Bible verse reminds me that everything about You is perfect in every way. Every word You speak in the Bible is pure—absolutely perfect. Every word You spoke in the past is true now, and it will be forever. When You say something, You mean it. There's no taking it back or need to change it. When You make a promise, that's it! I know that I can always trust Your words.

MORNING

## Stronger and Stronger

*They go from strength to strength.*

PSALM 84:7 KJV

Dear God, each day You make me a little stronger. It's not about body strength. You give me strength to face whatever is going to come up today. If it's something challenging with schoolwork, You'll give me strength to learn it. If it's strength to put up with someone or something that irritates me, You'll give me strength for that too. You lead me from strength to strength, just like this Bible verse says. Amen.

EVENING

## Dealing with Anger

*"In your anger do not sin": Do not let the sun go down while you are still angry.*

EPHESIANS 4:26 NIV

Heavenly Father, I need Your help dealing with my anger. Whether I'm just a bit annoyed, kind of angry, or totally furious, I want to handle those feelings in healthy ways. Help me not to allow any angry feelings to grow inside me. Help me to control my temper and talk calmly about what bothers me. Show me how to give my anger to You so I can live in peace. Amen.

MORNING

## Calm My Heart

*For God did not give us a spirit of fear. He gave us a spirit of power and of love and of a good mind.*

2 TIMOTHY 1:7 NLV

Dear God, please help me get rid of the fear that's bothering me as I come to You this morning. Calm my racing heart. Fill me up with Your strength and courage. What I have to do today seems much bigger than I can handle, but with You I can do anything. You have given me the spirit of power, love, and a quiet mind. Make me strong, Lord. Let's go!

EVENING

## God's Greatness

*The earth will be full of the knowledge of the LORD as the waters cover the sea.*

ISAIAH 11:9 NASB

Father God, my family took a road trip, and we saw many amazing things. The more I see of Your creation, the more I appreciate Your greatness. How did You ever create such magnificent things as mountains, canyons, gigantic waterfalls, oceans that stretch for miles, forests with trees that seem to touch the sky. . . ? I praise You, God! Your creativity is amazing—and it's all there for us to enjoy.

MORNING

## Be Happy with What You Have

*Be happy with what you have.*

Hebrews 13:5 NLV

God, it's so easy to break the tenth commandment: "You shall not covet. . .anything that belongs to your neighbor" (Exodus 20:17 NIV). It's a way of life in our world. We see stuff that others have, and we want it too. Toys, games, electronics, shoes, clothes, sports equipment, vacations—we want it all! You've warned us about loving money and stuff more than we love You. Keep me focused on You, Lord. I will be happy with what I have.

EVENING

## Taking Up My Cross

*If any man will come after me, let him deny himself, and take up his cross daily, and follow me.*

Luke 9:23 KJV

Following You isn't always easy, Jesus. Things that happen to me sometimes seem like more than I can handle. When that happens, remind me of You bearing Your cross and all the torture and mental anguish that went with it. Your cross represents all my trouble; and You are with me always, carrying the load for me. Thank You, Jesus!

MORNING

## With Jesus

*"Father, I want My followers You gave Me to be with Me where I am. Then they may see My shining-greatness which You gave Me because You loved Me before the world was made."*

JOHN 17:24 NLV

Dear Father God, as much as I wish I knew what the future holds, only You know what will happen. Instead of worrying about it or thinking about the future too much, I choose to simply follow You today, tomorrow, and forever. You have everything under control. The truth is, I don't really care where You lead me—as long as Jesus is there too. Amen.

EVENING

## Sharing the Scriptures

*You have known the Holy Writings since you were a child. They are able to give you wisdom that leads to being saved from the punishment of sin by putting your trust in Christ Jesus.*

2 TIMOTHY 3:15 NLV

God, You've been teaching me as I read Your Word and apply its teaching to my life. I'm becoming wiser about who You are and the wonderful things You do. Why am I keeping to myself what I'm learning? That's not what You want! Your Word is for sharing, and that's what I'm going to do. I will tell my friends about You and the Bible. I want them to know and love You too.

MORNING

## Joy

*For ye shall go out with joy, and be led forth with peace: the mountains and the hills shall break forth before you into singing, and all the trees of the field shall clap their hands.*

ISAIAH 55:12 KJV

Dear heavenly Father, I love this morning's Bible verse! How awesome that You're leading me into this day with joy and peace. I already feel like this is going to be a good day. As I go out the door this morning, I'm going to imagine the mountains and hills singing, "There she is!" and the trees and fields clapping their hands. I'm ready, God. Let's go.

EVENING

## Slow Down

*The plans of those who do their best lead only to having all they need, but all who are in a hurry come only to want.*

PROVERBS 21:5 NLV

Dear God, tonight's Bible verse gives me plenty to think about. When I take time to plan my work and do my best, things usually turn out well. But if I don't have a plan and I rush to get things done, my work is sloppy. When I haven't taken time to do my best, I end up not being happy with what I've done. Thanks for reminding me to slow down. Amen.

MORNING

## Under God's Command

*Let the rivers clap their hands, let the mountains sing together for joy.*

PSALM 98:8 NIV

Dear heavenly Father, I live near a river and the mountains. When snow melts in the mountains, it turns the trickling streams into a wild, rushing river. *Where does all that water go?* I wonder. When I look at the mountains, I look up toward You. Everything is under Your command, even the rushing river and those strong rocky mountains that seem to touch the sky. How great You are! Amen.

EVENING

## Out of Trouble!

*For [God] will take out of trouble the one in need when he cries for help, and the poor man who has no one to help.*

PSALM 72:12 NLV

God, You heard me yell, "Help!" and You sent someone right away to get me out of trouble. Maybe he was one of Your angels. I'm grateful that You are always watching over me. I'm sure You saw me about to get into trouble, and You were ready to rescue me even before I took that first step. Thank You, God. You are so good to me. Amen.

DAY 292

MORNING

# Let It Happen to Me

*Then Mary said, "I am willing to be used of the Lord. Let it happen to me as you have said."*
LUKE 1:38 NLV

Dear God, was Mary afraid when she heard You chose her to give birth to Your Son? What a huge responsibility. But she said, "Let it happen to me." Father, help me to be like Mary. If You have something for me to do that seems huge and too much, remind me of Mary's words. Let it happen to me. I know You'll give me strength to see it through. Amen.

EVENING

# His Awesome Power

*Say to God, "How awesome are your deeds! So great is your power. . . . All the earth bows down to you; they sing praise to you, they sing the praises of your name."*
PSALM 66:3–4 NIV

God, in the beginning there was nothing but You, and out of nothing You created the earth and everything in it. You made the sky, counted the stars, and gave them names. You tell the wind to stop, and it does. You quiet a raging sea. You've given sight to the blind and even raised the dead. Your power is awesome! Nothing is impossible for You. I bow to You, singing praises to Your name.

MORNING

## God Is Not a Vending Machine

*Ye ask, and receive not, because ye ask amiss, that ye may consume it upon your lusts.*

James 4:3 KJV

God, sometimes I treat You like a vending machine—tell the machine what I want, press buttons, and a snack comes out. I figure if I say the right words to You, I'll get what I want. Forgive me. I know You always give me what I need. My wants might not be what's best for me. So help me to ask for the right things—those that are in line with Your will. Amen.

EVENING

## Don't Give Up!

*We are glad for our troubles also. We know that troubles help us learn not to give up. When we have learned not to give up, it shows we have stood the test. When we have stood the test, it gives us hope.*

Romans 5:3–4 NLV

"Don't give up!" That's what my dad always tells me. So many times I wanted to give up, Father God, but Dad encouraged me to keep going. I'm glad I did, because I accomplished things I never thought I could. I learned important lessons along the way too. Thanks, God, for teaching me patience and determination and giving me the strength to follow through. And thanks for giving me my awesome dad. Amen.

MORNING

## Golden Words

*A word fitly spoken is like apples of gold in settings of silver.*

PROVERBS 25:11 NKJV

Heavenly Father, today I need some words spoken to me that remind me of all the good things I am. My self-esteem needs a boost. I'm not looking to be all that. I just want someone to tell me I'm awesome just the way I am. I know You think I'm awesome all the time. But today, please open my ears to compliments. Lift my spirits. Send some golden words my way. Amen.

EVENING

## The Bible Gives Me Hope

*For whatsoever things were written aforetime were written for our learning, that we through patience and comfort of the scriptures might have hope.*

ROMANS 15:4 KJV

Dear Father, the Bible gives me hope. When I'm sad, confused, frustrated, or lonely, I know I'll find answers, strength, and comfort by reading Your Word. The Bible teaches me how You want me to live. When I memorize scripture and apply it to my life, that leads me nearer to You. I know I can trust every word written in the Bible. I'm grateful, Father, for Your Word. Amen.

MORNING

## Take Hold of God's Word

*But My words and My statutes, which I commanded My servants the prophets, did they not overtake and take hold of your fathers? So they repented.*

ZECHARIAH 1:6 AMPC

God, I want everyone to take hold of Your Word, to believe in You and the Bible. I'm shy talking about You. I think I have to plan my words, but I don't. I'm not the one who opens the hearts of others to receive You. That's Your job. I'm the messenger who shares the good news about Jesus. Help me not to be shy. Lead me to those who need to know You. Amen.

EVENING

## Helped

*And the LORD shall help them and deliver them. . .because they trust in Him.*

PSALM 37:40 NKJV

You always pull me through trouble, God. You lead others to pitch in, and somehow even my biggest problems work themselves out. I have a part in getting myself out of trouble, but You are the one who smooths the way for me. Thank You for delivering me from my problems at just the right time. You are so great! I appreciate every bit of help You give me. Amen.

DAY 296

MORNING

# God Hears Me

*And this is the confidence that we have in him, that, if we ask any thing according to his will, he heareth us.*

1 JOHN 5:14 KJV

When I pray, Lord, I'm confident that You are always listening. You understand the thoughts behind my prayers even when I don't. I never feel like I'm speaking into the air to some imaginary friend. You are 100 percent real! I can tell You anything and have confidence that You will know and provide whatever I need. I love You, God. Thanks for being my very best friend. Amen.

EVENING

# Keeping God's Word

*Blessed is he that readeth, and they that hear the words of this prophecy, and keep those things which are written therein: for the time is at hand.*

REVELATION 1:3 KJV

Dear God, for as long as I live, I want to keep doing my best to live up to Your Word. I will try to follow Your commands, and I will put them to use to serve You. Please guide me in reading and living what's in the Bible. Help me to study and understand Your Word. Lead me to behave in ways that please You so I will be a good example for others.

MORNING

## In Jesus' Name

*Jesus saith unto him, I am the way, the truth, and the life: no man cometh unto the Father, but by me.*

JOHN 14:6 KJV

When I pray to You, God, I often pray using Jesus' name. The Bible says He is the Way and the Truth. Through Jesus, I find my way to the life You have planned for me. With Jesus' help, I stay on the right path. If I get off course, He finds me and brings me back. I choose to follow Your Son. Guide me in ways to lead others to follow Him too. Amen.

EVENING

## Tidings of Great Joy

*The angel said unto them, Fear not: for, behold, I bring you good tidings of great joy, which shall be to all people.*

LUKE 2:10 KJV

Dear heavenly Father, I love reading the Christmas story in the Bible, especially about the angels bringing good tidings of great joy—the good news that Jesus had been born. I want to share His story with everyone around me. At Christmas and always, provide me with opportunities to share the good news. Use me as You would an angel, proclaiming with great joy the news about Your Son. Amen.

MORNING

## A Joyful Noise

*Shout joyfully to the LORD, all the earth;*
*break forth in song, rejoice, and sing praises.*

PSALM 98:4 NKJV

Dear God, this morning I thank You for music! I love listening to it. You've also made me aware of music in nature: the sounds of raindrops on the rooftop, wind whistling through bare tree branches, birds singing, and river water bubbling around stones. Thank You, God, for choirs, worship bands, orchestras, and all kinds of musical instruments. May they lift up their joyful songs to praise You. Amen.

EVENING

## Joy in God's Word

*These things have I spoken unto you, that my joy might*
*remain in you, and that your joy might be full.*

JOHN 15:11 KJV

You are my guide and teacher, God. Your Word teaches me how to behave toward others and how to be a good example for them. It gives me everything I need to follow the path You've set for my life. It makes me strong and helps me conquer obstacles that get in my way. Your Word fills me up with all things good, and it brings me joy.

MORNING

## Working Together

*I say unto you, That if two of you shall agree on earth as touching any thing that they shall ask, it shall be done for them of my Father which is in heaven.*

MATTHEW 18:19 KJV

Thank You, God, for friends who share my faith. I'm glad we can worship and pray together. In our church youth group, we work together to help people in our community. We always begin by praying together, and I know You hear us. You are there with us. Help my friends and me to serve You. When we combine all the skills and talent You've given us, we can do some amazing things.

EVENING

## Sound Wisdom

*But the wisdom that is from above is first pure, then peaceable, gentle, and easy to be intreated, full of mercy and good fruits, without partiality, and without hypocrisy.*

JAMES 3:17 KJV

God, when I pray seeking Your wisdom, You are willing to provide it. I've learned to know sound wisdom—the kind that comes from You. Your wisdom gives me a peaceful feeling. Your wisdom is gentle. You don't criticize me for what I don't know; instead, You lead me to know and understand when You see that I'm ready. When I put into action the wisdom You give me, it always leads to something good.

MORNING

# Speak the Good News

*We also believe and therefore speak.*

2 CORINTHIANS 4:13 NKJV

God, when it comes to sharing the good news about Jesus, thank You that I don't need to know everything or have every answer. I don't have to be in some special place or make a speech. I don't have to be a pastor or go to school to learn how to share the good news. All You require is that I let go of my shyness and speak about what Jesus means to me.

EVENING

# My Safe Place and Strength

*God is our refuge and strength,*
*a very present help in trouble.*

PSALM 46:1 NKJV

Father God, if I need a safe place to rest, You are there. But don't allow me to stay too long. I don't want to use You to avoid things. Instead, I need to get out in the world and take chances. In my resting place, You give me advice to make wise decisions before I take a risk. You lead me and guide me. In my safe place, Lord, You give me strength. Amen.

MORNING

## Answered Prayers

*"If you get your life from Me and My Words live in you, ask whatever you want. It will be done for you."*
JOHN 15:7 NLV

Dear God, help me to remember Your words when I pray. Help me to keep my thoughts focused on You while I wait for answers to my prayers. Keep me close. Remind me that You love me and will answer me in the ways You know are best. It might not be what I want or expect, but I trust that Your answers are good. Hear my prayers, Lord, and answer me. Amen.

EVENING

## The Best Advice Ever

*The sweet smell of perfume and oils is pleasant, and so is good advice from a friend.*
PROVERBS 27:9 NCV

Dear Jesus, You are my best friend. Too often I jump right in, doing what I want without asking You for advice. You give the best advice ever! Remind me to come to You. Let me tell You my thoughts. Then help me to listen to Your wisdom. You are the friend who leads and guides me. You will never send me in the wrong direction. Thank You for being my friend. Amen.

DAY 302

MORNING

# Tossed by the Waves

*You must have faith as you ask Him.*
*You must not doubt. Anyone who doubts is like*
*a wave which is pushed around by the sea.*

JAMES 1:6 NLV

God, reading James 1:6 makes me think of myself in a small boat on the ocean. My worries are like waves tossing the boat around. I forget too often that You are the captain in charge of the boat. With You in control, I don't have to worry. You have all the power to calm the waves and keep me safe. Don't let me doubt You, God. Please build up my faith in You. Amen.

EVENING

# Blessings in Sadness

*"Blessed are those who mourn,*
*for they will be comforted."*

MATTHEW 5:4 NIV

Dear Lord Jesus, my family is very sad today. A good friend of ours died. We know he is in heaven with You, but still we are sad because we will miss him. You promise to bless and comfort us. I ask that You do that not only for my family but for everyone who loved our friend. He is happy and with You now. We know we will see him again. Amen.

MORNING

## With Endurance

*Indeed we count them blessed who endure. You have heard of the perseverance of Job and seen the end intended by the Lord—that the Lord is very compassionate and merciful.*

JAMES 5:11 NKJV

Dear Lord, my mom and I are doing a charity run next week. It's a three-mile run, and we've been training. I've built up endurance! At first I couldn't go very far without getting tired, but now I have confidence I can do the whole three miles. Thank You for reminding me to keep going. You're my trainer, the one who gets me over the rough spots and to the finish line. Thanks, God! Amen.

EVENING

## Laughter

*Then our mouth was filled with laughter and our tongue with joyful shouting.*

PSALM 126:2 NASB

Thank You, God, for things that make me laugh. Last night I watched a funny movie. I laughed so hard my sides ached. I think it makes You happy to see me having fun. Laughter is good unless it's laughing at someone. That's wrong and something we should never do. When I'm having fun with my friends and we're laughing and shouting with joy—those are the best times ever. Amen.

DAY 304

MORNING

## Moving Mountains

*For verily I say unto you, That whosoever shall say unto this mountain, Be thou removed, and be thou cast into the sea; and shall not doubt in his heart, but shall believe that those things which he saith shall come to pass; he shall have whatsoever he saith.*

MARK 11:23 KJV

Dear Jesus, You taught using examples. I don't want to throw any mountains into the ocean, and it's hard for me to believe that's what You really meant. Show me the truth of Your words. I know You want me to have enough faith to believe You have power to do *anything*. Build up my faith in You, and get rid of any doubt in my heart. Amen.

EVENING

## God Says, "Come to Me"

*In [Jesus] and through faith in him we may approach God with freedom and confidence.*

EPHESIANS 3:12 NIV

Lord Jesus, You made it possible for me to come to Your Father with a clean heart. You took all my sin away so the Father could welcome me in to talk with Him in prayer. He invites me in, promising I can come without the shame of sin filling my heart. Thanks to You, Jesus, Your Father has already forgiven me. When I pray, I have confidence that He hears me and loves me. Amen.

MORNING

# According to God's Will

*The prayer from the heart of a man right with God has much power.*

James 5:16 NLV

Dear God, when I ask You for something, I want to pray according to Your will. There are things I may want with all my heart; and when You won't give them to me, I wonder why. Maybe it's because what I'm asking for doesn't fit with Your plan for me. Please set my thoughts in line with Yours. Lead me to pray for what *You* want for me. Amen.

EVENING

# Hope and Loving-Kindness

*O Israel, hope in the Lord! For there is loving-kindness with the Lord. With Him we are saved for sure.*

Psalm 130:7 NLV

Dear God, tonight I'm grateful for hope. I kept on hoping You would help me finish that big project, and You did! It turned out even better than I'd hoped for. You always treat me with loving-kindness. When I felt like giving up, I had a talk with You, and You gave me strength and courage to keep going. When I lost faith in myself, You built up my confidence. I love You, Lord. Amen.

## DAY 306

### MORNING

# Be Courageous

*Be of good courage, and He shall strengthen your heart, all you who hope in the LORD.*

PSALM 31:24 NKJV

Heavenly Father, I'm not the most courageous person. I usually let others go first and see what happens, and then I'm willing to try. I want to be more courageous. I want to be the first one ready to try something new—to take a bite of sushi or touch that hairy spider when the zookeeper offers. Build my courage, Lord. Help me to be willing. Amen.

### EVENING

# Things Not Seen

*Now faith is the substance of things hoped for, the evidence of things not seen.*

HEBREWS 11:1 NKJV

Father, I wonder what wonderful things You have planned for my life that I can't see. Will I meet someone, fall in love, and have children one day? What sort of work have You planned for me? Where will I go? What will I see? I think a lot about the future. My faith and hope are in You, and I believe that whatever You have planned for me will be amazing. Amen.

MORNING

## Lessons in Trust

*I have put my trust in the Lord God,*
*that I may declare all Your works.*
Psalm 73:28 NKJV

Heavenly Father, teach me to trust. Even when I think I'm putting all my faith in You, I often find it hard to take that first step into something new. You know what's ahead of me. I want to trust You more that You will give me courage and strength to face the future. I want to trust that You'll keep me safe. I believe You already have everything under Your control. Amen.

EVENING

## Sadness into Joy

*And ye now therefore have sorrow: but I will*
*see you again, and your heart shall rejoice,*
*and your joy no man taketh from you.*
John 16:22 KJV

Dear Jesus, today's Bible verse is an important part of Your story. Your disciples were sad. You told them You were going away but that You would see them again. These men had walked and talked with You. You were their leader, their friend. How lost they must have felt when You died. But three days later. . . Wow, Lord! You turned their sadness into joy when You were alive again.

# DAY 308

MORNING

## Every Little Detail

*Agree with Him in all your ways,*
*and He will make your paths straight.*
PROVERBS 3:6 NLV

Dear God, You are present in every detail of my life. You know me inside and out. I take for granted the little things, like You directing every beat of my heart and knowing the number of hairs on my head and what I'm thinking even before I think it. I praise You for being ever-present in my life, and I want to honor You in all my ways. Amen.

EVENING

## All Through My Life

*"You have shown me the ways of life.*
*I will be full of joy when I see Your face."*
ACTS 2:28 NLV

Dear heavenly Father, I am young, and our relationship is just beginning to grow. You are teaching me, and I still have so much to learn. Show me the right path to take. Guide me through my life. I look forward to taking each step with You. And then, one day, maybe when I am very old, I will be filled with joy when I finally meet You face-to-face. Amen.

MORNING

## Willing Mind

*"Acknowledge the God of your father, and serve him with wholehearted devotion and with a willing mind, for the LORD searches every heart and understands every desire and every thought. If you seek him, he will be found by you."*

1 CHRONICLES 28:9 NIV

God, I'm guilty of doing whatever I want without thinking of what You want for me. Before I take that step onto a wrong path, remind me to think of You. Make my mind willing. Help me to trust that Your plans for me are better than my own. Set Your ways in my heart, and then lead me to walk toward You. Help me to agree with all Your ways for my life. Amen.

EVENING

## Do It for God

*And whatsoever ye do, do it heartily, as to the Lord, and not unto men; knowing that of the Lord ye shall receive the reward of the inheritance: for ye serve the Lord Christ.*

COLOSSIANS 3:23–24 KJV

Dear heavenly Father, I'm bored with my homework. I get bored if it's too easy or when the topic doesn't interest me. I need to remember that whatever I do, I should do it as if working for You. That means giving it my best all the time. If I get bored, please help me turn my thoughts toward You. I want to do my best to bring honor to You. Amen.

# DAY 310

## MORNING

# The Giver

*You open your hand and satisfy*
*the desires of every living thing.*

PSALM 145:16 NIV

Heavenly Father, You are so faithful to meet my needs. I want to help meet the needs of others. Maybe I can help provide food for the birds and animals. I can ask my parents to help me share gently used toys and clothes with kids in need. I can join in my church's activities to help the poor. Please show me other ways I might help. Amen.

## EVENING

# Peaceful Sleep

*In peace I will both lie down and sleep, for You, Lord,*
*alone make me dwell in safety and confident trust.*

PSALM 4:8 AMPC

Dear Lord, every night when I lie down, I feel You with me. You are the last one I talk with before I fall asleep. As I close my eyes, I feel You and Your angels watching over me. I know I am safe as I rest, because my trust is in You. Please give me sweet dreams, and help me to wake refreshed and ready to start a new day. Amen.

MORNING

## Perfect

*Let your heart therefore be perfect with the LORD our God, to walk in his statutes, and to keep his commandments, as at this day.*

1 KINGS 8:61 KJV

God, I'm a girl who wants to do everything perfectly. I'm never satisfied with my work. I keep making changes, trying to make it better. Please remind me that I don't live in a perfect world. Nothing is perfect, and no one is perfect except You. Help me to know when I've crossed the line from doing my best to trying to be perfect. What's important is that my heart is perfectly set on You.

EVENING

## Where Is Peace Found?

*For the kingdom of God is not a matter of eating and drinking, but of righteousness, peace and joy in the Holy Spirit, because anyone who serves Christ in this way is pleasing to God and receives human approval.*

ROMANS 14:17–18 NIV

Heavenly Father, people seem to be searching for peace these days. When they disagree and won't let go of their angry feelings, peace is hard to find. True peace comes when people ask You into their hearts and do their best to follow Your commands. I pray tonight for those looking for peace. May they find it in You and then live in peace with others. Amen.

MORNING

## Decisions

*If any of you lacks wisdom, you should ask God, who gives generously to all without finding fault, and it will be given to you.*

James 1:5 NIV

Dear Lord, it's so hard sometimes to know what Your will is. How can I know exactly what You want me to do? I have some choices to make today. I ask today that You give me wisdom. Send me guidance. Send a person, a thought, or a scripture to help me know what You are thinking. Lead me through this day. I want to honor You with each decision I make. Amen.

EVENING

## A Joyful Giver

*Remember the words of the Lord Jesus, how he said, It is more blessed to give than to receive.*

Acts 20:35 KJV

Father, sometimes I don't feel like being a helper. People keep asking me to help with things at school and at church. Can't I just focus on myself sometimes? When I feel this way, remind me that whenever I give my time to others, I'm being Your servant—Your helper here in the world. I know it's okay to take a break sometimes, but please make me a joyful giver the rest of the time. Amen.

MORNING

## Celebration

*They celebrate your abundant goodness and joyfully sing of your righteousness.*

Psalm 145:7 NIV

Dear Jesus, I love celebrating Your goodness. Christmas, when You left heaven to come to earth as a baby, and Easter, when You came to life after dying on the cross, are my favorite times to celebrate. I love singing Christmas songs about the day You were born and being in my church Christmas plays. And at Easter I'm super happy and thankful because You made a way for me to live with You in heaven one day. Jesus, there's so much joy in knowing You! Amen.

EVENING

## Joyful in Hope

*Happy is he that hath the God of Jacob for his help, whose hope is in the Lord his God.*

Psalm 146:5 KJV

Dear God, each day I realize even more that joy and hope go together. I have joy because my hope is in You. Thank You, Lord, that as Your child, I don't go through the day feeling hopeless. No matter what happens, I can find joy because my hope isn't based on whatever situation I'm in. I know You have good plans for me. My hope is in You! Amen.

DAY 314

MORNING

# Because I Want To

*"O my God, I know that You test the heart and are pleased with what is right. I have given these things because I have wanted to with a clean heart. And now I have seen with joy how Your people who are here give gifts to You because they want to."*

1 CHRONICLES 29:17 NLV

Dear God, I follow Your commands because I want to. I know that everything I have is because of You. Each day You bless me in ways both big and small. All I can give You is my love and my promise that I'll try my best to please You. I want to please You, God. Show me anything I'm holding back. I want You to have it all. Amen.

EVENING

# Be Considerate

*You know this, my beloved brothers and sisters. Now everyone must be quick to hear, slow to speak, and slow to anger.*

JAMES 1:19 NASB

Heavenly Father, I know I can be more considerate of others. Forgive me for when I haven't been. I sometimes think of myself instead of someone else. Help me to listen when others are speaking to me. Show me what You want me to say when I answer them, and help me choose my words wisely. And if we disagree, help me to consider their feelings instead of getting angry. Amen.

## MORNING

# I Surrender!

*But now, O LORD, You are our Father; we are the clay, and You our potter; and all we are the work of Your hand.*

ISAIAH 64:8 NKJV

God, there's a war going on inside me about right and wrong. My friends do things that I know don't please You. Sometimes I want to go along with them because those things don't seem so bad to me. But God, You are the one who guides me. When I feel a tug-of-war in my heart, I surrender to You. Show me the way, and give me strength to follow what You say is right.

## EVENING

# Tiny Things

*"If anyone gives even a cup of cold water to one of these little ones who is my disciple, truly I tell you, that person will certainly not lose their reward."*

MATTHEW 10:42 NIV

Dear heavenly Father, thanks for reminding me that no act of kindness is too small. Holding the door for someone, helping to carry bags of groceries, sharing a treat with a friend—You see the little things I do, and they make You glad. Tiny acts of kindness add up. Help me to reach out to others. Open my eyes to more small ways I can help. Amen.

MORNING

## My Friend but My God

*O Lord, who may live in Your tent? Who may live on Your holy hill? He who walks without blame and does what is right and good, and speaks the truth in his heart.*

PSALM 15:1–2 NLV

Father, I enjoy a personal relationship with You. But I need to remember that it's unlike any personal relationship I have on earth. You want me to remember Your power and greatness. I'm not deserving of the many ways You bless me. With every breath I take, You want me to honor and praise You. I will remember that You are not only my friend but my almighty God, Creator of the universe. Amen.

EVENING

## God Moments

*By love serve one another. For all the law is fulfilled in one word, even in this; thou shalt love thy neighbour as thyself.*

GALATIANS 5:13–14 KJV

Dear God, sometimes I forget that my life is not all about me! Serving You is what this life is about. Father, guide me to show love to others today. Make every moment a "God moment," with You opening my eyes to the many needs around me. Give me a heart that loves others and puts them ahead of myself. I'm ready to start my day. Let's go! Amen.

MORNING

## Work in Progress

*For the eyes of the Lord are on the righteous*
*and his ears are attentive to their prayer.*
1 PETER 3:12 NIV

Father God, I'm amazed that You never get tired of listening to me. You hear me speak about the same fears, complaints, and problems day after day. My work overcoming them seems slow; but You are patient with me, and I'm making progress. Thank You for how You continue to work in me: so faithfully, patiently, and lovingly. Lead me from being this girl toward becoming the woman You want me to be. Amen.

EVENING

## Use Me, Lord

*For whosoever will save his life shall lose it;*
*but whosoever shall lose his life for my sake*
*and the gospel's, the same shall save it.*
MARK 8:35 KJV

Dear Jesus, I feel like the ways I'm trying to serve You aren't big enough or important enough. Maybe the small ways I try to help are all You desire from me right now. But as I get older, I want You to use me in bigger ways. How can I serve You to really make a difference in the world? Show me the way. Use me to lead others to You. Amen.

DAY 318

MORNING

## Bring Us Together, Lord

*That ye may with one mind and one mouth glorify God, even the Father of our Lord Jesus Christ.*

ROMANS 15:6 KJV

Father God, I know You want us all to get along. There seems to be so many people disagreeing lately. Please, will You help us come together? Give me patience with others. Make me slow to get angry. And before I allow myself to get upset, remind me to try to see things through the eyes of others. Bring us together, Lord, in ways that glorify You and bring You honor.

EVENING

## Thankful Hearts

*Thou shalt rejoice in every good thing which the LORD thy God hath given unto thee, and unto thine house, thou, and the Levite, and the stranger that is among you.*

DEUTERONOMY 26:11 KJV

Dear God, thank You for blessing me and my family. Too often I think about what we don't have or what I want. Please remind me to be forever grateful. I don't want to take for granted the many little ways You bless us every day. Thank You for providing us with what we need and for loving us all the time. Help us to be aware of Your presence and to have thankful hearts. Amen.

MORNING

## Believing

*Be not faithless, but believing.*
John 20:27 KJV

I believe in You, Jesus. I believe in Your power, wisdom, and love. I believe that when You died on the cross, You took away my sins and made me ready to be in God's presence. I want everything I do to reflect the thanks and honor You deserve. Teach me to trust You even more and to believe the Bible's truths. Remind me to share You with others so they will believe in You too.

EVENING

## Bless This House

*My people will live in peaceful dwelling places, in secure homes, in undisturbed places of rest.*
Isaiah 32:18 NIV

Dear heavenly Father, please bless this house and everyone in it. May this always be my family's place of safety, comfort, and peace. Guard us from any harm. Protect us from bringing home trouble and disagreements that get in the way of our happiness. Fill up our home with Your love so each member of our family may feel Your presence here. Shower Your blessings down on us like rain. Amen.

DAY 320

MORNING

## Endurance Required

*Let us run with endurance the race that is set before us.*

HEBREWS 12:1 NKJV

Endurance. Sometimes it's hard to keep going. I easily get bored. If there's something I *have* to do, I poke along, feeling like I want to give up. We all have to do things we don't want to. So give me strength to endure those things. Give me a mindset to keep working at them and to do a good job. Remind me that with everything I do, God, I'm working for You. Amen.

EVENING

## Don't Give Up on Jesus

*"The Father sent Me. He did not want Me to lose any of all those He gave Me. He wants Me to raise them to life on the last day."*

JOHN 6:39 NLV

Dear Jesus, some people accept You as their Lord and Savior, but that's all. If they don't think about You and work at following You, their love for You grows cold. It's easy then for them to slip back to taking the wrong path and doing things that don't please You. Do I know someone like that? If I do, Lord, lead me to them, and show me how to guide them back to You.

MORNING

## His-Story

*He has made everything beautiful in its time.*
*He has also set eternity in the human heart; yet no one can fathom what God has done from beginning to end.*

ECCLESIASTES 3:11 NIV

Dear God, I wish I could time travel from the beginning when You created everything until now. What would I see? I think some of the history would be ugly, but then I would see how You always make things beautiful in Your own time. History is Your story, God. I'm living in the middle of it. You are the only one who knows what's in the future and how it will end.

EVENING

## Stressed Out

*A heart at peace gives life to*
*the body, but envy rots the bones.*

PROVERBS 14:30 NIV

Heavenly Father, please give me a peaceful heart. Stress finds a way of creeping into my heart and taking away my peace. I get stressed out when there's too much to do, when I get frustrated, when I'm worried about something, and even if I want something I can't have. I know stress isn't good for me. So please, God, take away the stress, and fill me up with Your peace. Amen.

DAY 322

## MORNING

# Wake UP!

*"The joy of the Lord is your strength."*
NEHEMIAH 8:10 NIV

Dear Lord, some mornings I wake up ready to go. Other mornings, like this one, I just want to stay in bed. Remind me that, as Your child, I can tap into Your power source to give myself strength. I might not always feel joyful, but I'm hopeful that, with You by my side, I'll get through the day. It's time for me to get out of bed. Give me strength, Lord! Amen.

## EVENING

# Two Are Better Than One

*Two are better than one; because they have a good reward for their labour. For if they fall, the one will lift up his fellow.*
ECCLESIASTES 4:9–10 KJV

Father God, thank You for my "buddy." Our teacher put us in buddy pairs to work together on a science project. My buddy is amazing. She has skills different from mine, and together we make a great team. Working together with someone makes the time go by fast, and it's more fun. When I read tonight's Bible verse, it made me think of her. Two really are better than one! Amen.

MORNING

## True Joy

*These things have I spoken unto you, that my joy might remain in you, and that your joy might be full.*

JOHN 15:11 KJV

Dear Father God, I think true joy comes when we trust in Your words in the Bible, love You, and follow Your commands. Add to that all the fun things You bring to us—friends, new places to explore, celebrations, special treats, activities—all of it put together fills our hearts with joy! Thank You, Father, for the many blessings that add fun and laughter to our lives. Amen.

EVENING

## A Covering of Faith

*Most important of all, you need a covering of faith in front of you. This is to put out the fire-arrows of the devil.*

EPHESIANS 6:16 NLV

Heavenly Father, I'm learning that faith is like a shield—that big metal thing ancient warriors held in front of their bodies to protect themselves from arrows. If my faith in You is strong, I have protection from whatever tries to harm me. All I need to do is trust You and have faith that You will take care of me. My faith is in You, Lord. You are my protector.

MORNING

## First Things First

*"For where your treasure is,*
*there your heart will be also."*
MATTHEW 6:21 NIV

Dear God, I need help with priorities—putting the most important things first. It's so easy for them to get out of whack. Show me the things I've let creep to the top that don't belong there. Then guide me to replace them with things that need more of my attention. At the top of my list, Father, is spending time with You. Tell me, what comes next? Amen.

EVENING

## Friends Help Each Other

*If either of them falls down, one can help the other up.*
*But pity anyone who falls and has no one to help them up.*
ECCLESIASTES 4:10 NIV

Dear God, I want to become more of a giver. Guide me to notice when a friend needs my help. I want to be aware, because she might be embarrassed or uncomfortable asking for help. Open my eyes to the needs of my friends, and then show me the best way to react. Whether their needs are big or small, I want to be the kind of friend who is always ready to help. Amen.

MORNING

## Don't Worry!

*Don't worry about anything, but pray about everything.*
PHILIPPIANS 4:6 CEV

Dear Jesus, why do I continue to worry? The Bible tells me again and again that I don't have to worry, because You have everything under control. I can give all my troubles to You and trust You to work everything out. Worry isn't good for me. It doesn't lead to anything good. So, Lord, once more I give my problems to You in faith that everything is going to be all right. Amen.

EVENING

## Fighting Discouragement

*"You will have success if you are careful to observe the decrees and laws that the LORD gave Moses for Israel. Be strong and courageous. Do not be afraid or discouraged."*
1 CHRONICLES 22:13 NIV

Jesus, I'm discouraged. I keep trying my best, and I'm working hard, but I just can't seem to overcome these empty feelings. I need You to replace them with something better, something brighter. You remind me that You will give me strength, so I have no reason to let discouragement rule my heart. When I feel weak, Your power can fill me up. So please give me strength to keep going. Amen.

# DAY 326

MORNING

## Extras

*My God will meet all your needs according to the riches of his glory in Christ Jesus.*

PHILIPPIANS 4:19 NIV

Dear heavenly Father, I'm so grateful for all the ways You provide for my needs. Sometimes Your blessings even go beyond what I need. Thank You for those surprises! You always know when I can use a little something extra. When You give me more than I need, help me to remember that I can share some of it with others. God, You are so good to me! Amen.

EVENING

## The Patience Challenge

*Love is patient, love is kind.*

1 CORINTHIANS 13:4 NIV

My love isn't always patient and kind, Lord. Sometimes the way others behave toward me challenges my patience, and then I find myself behaving badly too. You are always patient, kind, and caring toward me. Even when I haven't deserved it, You've offered me second chances. Beginning today, I'm going to challenge myself to be more patient with others. I want to become more like You. Will You help me, please? Amen.

MORNING

## Stuff Worth Nothing

*He who loves money will never have enough money to make him happy. It is the same for the one who loves to get many things. This also is for nothing.*

ECCLESIASTES 5:10 NLV

Dear God, I don't want to be someone who always wants more. Some people have tons of stuff, and still they're not happy. Stuff doesn't buy happiness. If I compare it to the kind of happiness that comes from You, it's worth nothing. You make me rich by putting all sorts of goodness in my heart—things like love, kindness, and caring. I'd rather have all those good things instead of more stuff. Amen.

EVENING

## Joyful All the Time

*Rejoice evermore. Pray without ceasing. In every thing give thanks: for this is the will of God in Christ Jesus concerning you.*

1 THESSALONIANS 5:16–18 KJV

Heavenly Father, help me to be joyful and happy every day. Each day is a gift from You. Remind me of that on days when I'm bored or when things aren't going the way I want them to. I'm thankful, God, for Your many blessings. Forgive me when I don't seem grateful. Your goodness is all around me. In all circumstances, Father, give me a joyful, thankful heart. Amen.

DAY 328

## MORNING

# Lost and Found

*"I tell you, My Father in heaven does not want one of these little children to be lost."*

MATTHEW 18:14 NLV

Dear Jesus, I feel so safe with You. I know You are always with me and watching over me. If I start walking down the wrong path in life, I'm sure You won't allow me to get lost. Even if I don't feel You nearby, I trust You to come, find me, and lead me home. You care for me, Jesus, always and in the best possible ways. I love You. Amen.

## EVENING

# I'm So Lovely!

*Your beauty should come from the inside. It should come from the heart. This is the kind that lasts. Your beauty should be a gentle and quiet spirit. In God's sight this is of great worth and no amount of money can buy it.*

1 PETER 3:4 NLV

Dear God, I'm glad You live inside my heart. Every day, I grow nearer to You. I feel You working on me, making me better all the time. There's a peacefulness inside me, a confidence that tells me I'm lovely both inside and out. It's nothing I'm doing by myself, Lord. It's Your beauty shining through me. When others look at me, I want them to see You. Amen.

MORNING

## The Only Way

*"Salvation is found in no one else, for there is no other name under heaven given to mankind by which we must be saved."*

ACTS 4:12 NIV

Jesus, You are the only one who saves us from our sins and leads us to live in heaven. Some people don't believe that. They think they must earn their way into heaven by doing good things. Others say they aren't sure You are God's Son. I'm sure You are Jesus, the Son of God, and I believe You want everyone to know that trusting in You is the only way to heaven. Amen.

EVENING

## The Gift of Salvation

*For the grace of God has appeared that offers salvation to all people.*

TITUS 2:11 NIV

Dear Father God, *salvation* is a word that means "being saved." Jesus saves us from being punished for our sins. What a wonderful gift that is! Your only Son gave His life to save all people who will put their trust in Him. Instead of having to earn our way to heaven, when we accept Jesus as our Savior, we are promised the gift of life forever in heaven when we die. Thank You, God, for Your Son and the gift of salvation. Amen.

MORNING

# God's Plan for Me

*He is the One Who saved us from the punishment of sin. He is the One Who chose us to do His work. It is not because of anything we have done. But it was His plan from the beginning that He would give us His loving-favor through Christ Jesus.*

2 TIMOTHY 1:9 NLV

Father, even before You made me, You had a wonderful plan for my life. You knew that when You called me, I would accept Jesus into my heart and be saved. Before I was born, You knew that when my life here on earth ended, I would be with You forever in heaven. I can't imagine how much You loved me to allow Your Son to suffer and die so I can be with You forever. Thank You, God!

EVENING

# Much More to Learn

*"Call to Me, and I will answer you, and show you great and mighty things, which you do not know."*

JEREMIAH 33:3 NKJV

Heavenly Father, as I read my Bible, I understand more about You and the mighty things You do. The Bible is teaching me the ways You want me to behave and how to get along with others. There is so much more I need to learn, and I know You will be my teacher for the rest of my life. I can't wait to discover what You plan to show me next. Amen.

MORNING

## A Friend in Need

*The next day we landed at Sidon; and Julius, in kindness to Paul, allowed him to go to his friends so they might provide for his needs.*

ACTS 27:3 NIV

Lord, You have a way of bringing people into our lives who help meet our needs. You use people to work out Your plans. Most of the time, they don't know that it's You moving them about, putting them in the right places at the right times to be of help. Thank You, God, for sending friends when I need them. And thank You too for sending me to help when someone else needs a friend.

EVENING

## My Strength and Shield

*The LORD is my strength and my shield; my heart trusts in him, and he helps me. My heart leaps for joy, and with my song I praise him.*

PSALM 28:7 NIV

Lord God, You give me strength to get past any obstacles that stand in my way. Your mighty power is like a shield that protects me. When I put all my trust in You, I know I can always count on You for help. When I remember that I'm Your child and I count all the ways You bless me, my heart leaps for joy. God, I praise You! Amen.

DAY 332

## MORNING

# Compassion

*The Lord is gracious and compassionate,*
*slow to anger and rich in love.*
Psalm 145:8 NIV

Dear God, *compassion* means caring deeply about the feelings of others. Please fill up my heart with compassion. I want a heart that truly loves and is caring and kind. I want to be a blessing to others, especially those who are lonely or hurting. Help me to be compassionate in the ways You are—gracious, slow to anger, and rich in love. Open my eyes to those who need a little compassion today. Amen.

## EVENING

# Our Heavenly Father

*As a father has compassion on his children,*
*so the Lord has compassion on those who fear him.*
Psalm 103:13 NIV

God, You are my heavenly Father. You have even more love and power than my dad here on earth. My dad knows a lot, but there are things he can't do. You, God, can do anything! The cool thing is that You are my dad's heavenly Father too. We both put our trust in You. We believe You understand us. You have compassion for us. You are our Father who blesses us and gives us strength.

MORNING

## Power over the World

*"I have told you these things so you may have peace in Me. In the world you will have much trouble. But take hope! I have power over the world!"*

JOHN 16:33 NLV

Dear Jesus, this morning, I pray for peace around the world. John 16:33 gives me hope. You tell us that You have power over the world and that true peace comes from knowing You. I believe it, Jesus. You always tell the truth. My faith and trust are in You. I'll do my best to live in peace with everyone while continuing to pray for peace on earth. Amen.

EVENING

## Never Give Up

*My Christian friends, you have obeyed me when I was with you. You have obeyed even more when I have been away. You must keep on working to show you have been saved from the punishment of sin. . . . [God] is working in you. God is helping you obey Him. God is doing what He wants done in you.*

PHILIPPIANS 2:12–13 NLV

Dear heavenly Father, I do my best to behave in ways that please You. I'm not perfect; and when I mess up, You always forgive me. Thank You for that. I'll never give up trying to do what's right. I'm Your work in progress. I'm grateful that You're forming me into a person You will use to do Your work here on earth. Amen.

MORNING

## Trust Your Work to the Lord

*Trust your work to the Lord,
and your plans will work out well.*
PROVERBS 16:3 NLV

Dear Lord, today I have to give a presentation. You know I don't like speaking in front of the class. I've worked really hard on my presentation, and last night I rehearsed it with my family. They said I did a great job! I'm putting all my trust in You today. Will You please help me to be brave? With You by my side, I know things will work out well. Amen.

EVENING

## Better Than Rubies

*For wisdom is better than rubies; and all the things
that may be desired are not to be compared to it.*
PROVERBS 8:11 KJV

Father God, I wasn't sure I knew what rubies were, so I looked for photos. What beautiful bright red stones You created. I love them! I found out that rubies are precious stones and very expensive. The Bible says that everything we desire, even the most amazing, precious stones, can't be compared to the wisdom that comes from You. Make me wise, Father. I want Your kind of wisdom. Amen.

MORNING

## Who's the Boss?

*In God I trust and am not afraid. What can man do to me? I am under vows to you, my God; I will present my thank offerings to you.*

PSALM 56:11–12 NIV

Dear God, I've been having a problem with one of my coaches. She's hard on me. I wish she were kinder when she tries to correct me. Help me to recognize that she's the one in charge and to be respectful. God, You're the boss of everyone, so maybe You could guide her to be a little nicer when she tries to help. Thank You. Amen.

EVENING

## Fervent Prayer

*The effective, fervent prayer of a righteous man avails much.*

JAMES 5:16 NKJV

Dear Father God, a "fervent prayer" is a prayer that comes from strong feelings in someone's heart. My prayers are fervent when there's something I really, *really* want from You. Those prayers are filled with so much feeling that my heart can barely hold it all. Along with asking for what I desire, I want some of my fervent prayers to be for others. So many people need Your help today. Amen.

DAY 336

MORNING

## I'm Content

*I am not saying this because I am in need, for I have learned to be content whatever the circumstances.*

PHILIPPIANS 4:11 NIV

Good morning, Father. I don't need anything today other than the blessings You have planned for me. I'm content with what I have. Even before I ask, You know what I need, and You're ready to provide it. I'm content knowing that You love me, are watching over me, and care for me all the time. I feel safe with You, God. So let's head out and begin this day. Amen.

EVENING

## A Little Meekness, Please

*With all lowliness and meekness, with longsuffering, forbearing one another in love.*

EPHESIANS 4:2 KJV

Heavenly Father, I like the way You're shaping my personality. Would You also add a little meekness to who I'm becoming? Meekness is a kind of quiet strength. Sometimes it means staying silent when I have strong feelings and want to speak. It also means quietly accepting Your will for me even when I don't like it. Lord, please guide me. Show me what it means to be meek. Amen.

MORNING

# People Pleaser

*Am I now trying to win the approval of human beings, or of God? Or am I trying to please people? If I were still trying to please people, I would not be a servant of Christ.*

GALATIANS 1:10 NIV

Dear God, I've learned something new. What I've learned is that if I work hard to please You, then most of the time I'm pleasing the people around me. When I put good behavior into action, those around me notice. And if I do my best work for You, then others are pleased with my work too. I don't have to be a people pleaser, Father, because pleasing others comes from pleasing You. Amen.

EVENING

# His Love Lasts Forever

*Prophecy and speaking in unknown languages and special knowledge will become useless. But love will last forever!*

1 CORINTHIANS 13:8 NLT

Father, our youth pastor asked us to define *forever* without mentioning time. Forever is hard to imagine. One of my friends defined forever as heaven. Another said forever is God. None of us said forever is love. But the Bible says Your love is forever. Your love and everything else about You are forever. You have no beginning and no end. Because of Your love, someday when I get to heaven, I will be "forever" too.

# DAY 338

## MORNING

# Give It to God

*Do not be anxious about anything,*
*but in every situation, by prayer and petition,*
*with thanksgiving, present your requests to God.*

PHILIPPIANS 4:6 NIV

Lord, all the stuff I need to do this week is swirling around me like a swarm of bees. I feel anxious. I just wish all of it was already done. This morning I give You my anxiety and stress. Cover me with Your peace, and guard my heart against worry. I know that if I take things one step at a time, everything will get done. I trust You, God, to help me. Amen.

## EVENING

# I'M Not Alone

*"Be strong and of good courage, do not fear nor be afraid*
*of them; for the LORD your God, He is the One who goes*
*with you. He will not leave you nor forsake you."*

DEUTERONOMY 31:6 NKJV

It would be so easy to give up, God, but You remind me I'm not in this alone. You are right beside me. I don't have to worry or be afraid, because You will stand up with me against anything that gets in my way. When I put all my trust in You, I know I'm safe. You'll give me all the strength I need to do what I have to do. Amen.

MORNING

## More Responsibility

*"Well done, my good and faithful servant. You have been faithful in handling this small amount, so now I will give you many more responsibilities. Let's celebrate together!"*

MATTHEW 25:23 NLT

Dear God, I've been wanting my parents to give me more responsibility, to sometimes let me stay home by myself for a little while when they go out. They worry about me, but I know how to be safe at home. They can trust me! Matthew 25:23 reminds me that if I show them I'm responsible with small things, then maybe they'll trust me with bigger things. Thanks for the reminder. Amen.

EVENING

## I Don't Know Everything

*Trust in the LORD with all thine heart;*
*and lean not unto thine own understanding.*

PROVERBS 3:5 KJV

Father God, I'm sorry for acting like a know-it-all. I thought I knew what I was doing, but then I found out that I didn't. I really messed things up. I should have thought before I started down the wrong path. I understand now that I was just getting in the way of Your will for me. I trust You, God. Set me on the right path, and let's try this again.

# DAY 340

### MORNING

## The Work of My Hands

*The LORD your God will bless you in all your harvest and in all the work of your hands, and your joy will be complete.*

DEUTERONOMY 16:15 NIV

God, my Creator, I haven't thought much about how much my hands help me do my work. I use them to type assignments on my computer, to set the table and help fold laundry, to put food in my dog's dish, to play volleyball, and even to get myself dressed, brush my teeth, and keep myself clean. Thank You for my hands, God. Please bless the work they do. Amen.

### EVENING

## Prayer Power

*The LORD is far from the wicked,*
*but He hears the prayer of the righteous.*

PROVERBS 15:29 NKJV

Dear Lord, talking with You in prayer gives power to my life. When I turn to You in trouble, I'm automatically connected with Your strength. You might not answer my prayers right away; but when You answer, You often give me something more or better than I asked for. You always listen when I pray, and You're ready to give me Your power whenever I need it. Thank You, Lord! Amen.

MORNING

## A Better Attitude

*Do everything without complaining and arguing.*

PHILIPPIANS 2:14 NLT

Dear God, my brother and I are supposed to work together today to clean out the garage. He keeps complaining, and we've been arguing all morning. I guess I've been doing a little complaining too. Neither of us wants to do this job, but we have to get it done. I'm asking You right now to help me have a better attitude. If I stay positive, maybe my brother will too. Amen.

EVENING

## My Five Senses

*For in him we live, and move, and have our being.*

ACTS 17:28 KJV

Lord God, thank You for the five senses: sight, sound, smell, taste, and touch. You could have designed a virtual world, but instead You created one that can be experienced. I'm so used to having five senses that I don't take time to appreciate them. I promise to be more aware and more grateful to You that I can see, hear, smell, taste, and touch things. Thank You, Father. Amen.

DAY 342

## MORNING

# Criticism

*Fools show their annoyance at once,*
*but the prudent overlook an insult.*
PROVERBS 12:16 NIV

Lord, I don't like being criticized. Nobody does. A certain girl is always putting me down. I feel like I want to criticize her back. Instead, Lord, help me keep my cool and stay quiet. Heal my heart of the words she's said, and give me patience. I know what she says about me isn't true. I'm going to pray that You will lead her to be kind. Amen.

## EVENING

# Gossip

*Put out of your life all. . .bad talk which hurts other*
*people, and bad feelings which hurt other people.*
EPHESIANS 4:31 NLV

Dear Father God, before I even knew it, I was spreading gossip about a kid at school. My friends and I got together. We were talking about stuff that went on in class, and I repeated something I'd heard about one of our classmates. I'm sorry, God. I know it's wrong to talk about others when it doesn't make them look good. Please forgive me, and help me do better next time. Amen.

MORNING

## Turnaround Thoughts

*Let God transform you into a new person by changing the way you think. Then you will learn to know God's will for you, which is good and pleasing and perfect.*

ROMANS 12:2 NLT

Dear God, I need to turn around my thoughts. They've been in the wrong places lately. I've been thinking about things I want that I don't have. I've been thinking that I'm annoyed with my family, teacher, and friends. I've even been thinking that I don't care if I don't always obey all the rules. God, I want my thoughts to change. Will You help me change the way I think? Amen.

EVENING

## The Good Things He Does for Me

*Let all that I am praise the LORD; may I never forget the good things he does for me. He forgives all my sins and heals all my diseases.*

PSALM 103:2–3 NLT

Father, when was the last time I praised You for all the good things You do for me? I pray, talking with You about all kinds of things, but I don't always remember to praise You. Thank You, Father, for the many good things You do for me. Thank You for forgiving my sins and keeping me safe and well. I praise You, God, not just for *some* things but for *everything*! Amen.

MORNING

# Spirit of God

*"I have filled him with the Spirit of God, giving him great wisdom, ability, and expertise in all kinds of crafts."*
EXODUS 31:3 NLT

Creator God, thank You that Your Holy Spirit is always at work in my heart. He gives me the power to learn and do many different things. He even helps me become an expert at some of them. I like today's verse because it mentions crafts. I'm crafty, God. Some of what I've made has even won prizes. I'm grateful for the help the Holy Spirit provides. Amen.

EVENING

# The Earth

*God said unto them, Be fruitful, and multiply, and replenish the earth, and subdue it: and have dominion over the fish of the sea, and over the fowl of the air, and over every living thing that moveth upon the earth.*
GENESIS 1:28 KJV

Heavenly Father, from the beginning of time, You've made clear what You want us to do. You want us to care for the earth in ways that please You. I want to learn what I can about Your creation so I can appreciate even more how wonderful it is. Then, Lord, I want to do whatever I can to keep it looking wonderful. Show me the way. Amen.

MORNING

## Whose Fault Is It?

*Make allowance for each other's faults, and forgive anyone who offends you. Remember, the Lord forgave you, so you must forgive others.*

COLOSSIANS 3:13 NLT

Father God, my sister and I argued over something last night, and I said, "It's all your fault!" As soon as I said it, I was sorry. I know You don't want us finding fault and blaming each other. I apologized to her, and I'm apologizing to You too. Please forgive me for losing my temper and hurting her feelings. I forgive her too for her part in our disagreement. Amen.

EVENING

## Tiny Faith

*"And whatever you ask in prayer, believing, you will receive it all."*

MATTHEW 21:22 NASB

Lord, I believe in You and I trust You, but how much I believe and trust changes. When I get the answers to prayer that I want, my faith is big. But when You make me wait for an answer, my faith level drops until it's tiny. I'm sorry, God. You know what's best for me. You love me and will answer my prayers in Your time and Your way. Please help my faith to grow.

MORNING

## Praise Ways

*He hath put a new song in my mouth, even praise unto our God: many shall see it, and fear, and shall trust in the LORD.*

PSALM 40:3 KJV

God, in church I learned there are many ways to praise You. I can praise You with the words I speak when I pray. I can sing praise songs to You, play worship songs using musical instruments, or dance to honor You. I can praise You together with my friends when we talk about all the great things You do. Please show me other ways I can honor You with praise. Amen.

EVENING

## Shut-Ins

*"I was in prison and you came to visit me."*

MATTHEW 25:36 NIV

Heavenly Father, some people are shut in their homes and unable to go outside and have fun. Maybe they are hurt or sick and are recovering at home. Some are old people who can't get out much, or maybe they live in a nursing home. Lord, show me. Are there shut-ins I could visit today? Give me some ideas about how I can bring some sunshine into their lives. Amen.

MORNING

## My Morning Prayer

*Listen to my cry for help, my King and my God. For I pray to you. In the morning, O Lord, You will hear my voice. In the morning I will lay my prayers before You and will look up.*

PSALM 5:2–3 NLV

Dear God, my morning prayer starts almost the same every day: "Lord, help me through this day." I ask for Your help; but I know that even if I didn't, You would be with me, helping me all the time. You hear me when I pray, and You also hear my every thought. How great is that! You love me. You take care of me. And You lead me. Amen.

EVENING

## Music

*Whatsoever ye do, do all to the glory of God.*

1 CORINTHIANS 10:31 KJV

Heavenly Father, I've been thinking today about the music I listen to. There are so many different music styles and performers to choose from. I want to choose music with lyrics that You find pleasing. What I listen to affects my attitude, my mood, and my behavior. Help me to be wise with my choices. I don't want the music I choose to go against what You're trying to do in me. Amen.

## DAY 348

MORNING

# The Lord Is My Shepherd

*He makes me lie down in green pastures,*
*he leads me beside quiet waters.*
PSALM 23:2 NIV

Dear God, I love the Twenty-Third Psalm. It starts, "The LORD is my shepherd; I shall not want" (verse 1 KJV). I imagine You watching over me and keeping me safe. I imagine myself resting in a pasture of soft green grass near a quiet stream. I have food, water, a safe place to live. . . Wait! I'm not just imagining it, God. You provide all those things for me and more. Thank You, my Lord and my shepherd.

EVENING

# A Little Help, Please

*In all thy ways acknowledge him,*
*and he shall direct thy paths.*
PROVERBS 3:6 KJV

I'm struggling tonight, Jesus. I need to finish this assignment, and my brain isn't cooperating. I'm thinking about everything but the words I need to write on this page. I'm sitting here at the table staring blankly into space. I know You want me to keep going and do my best. Jesus, I need Your help. Please give me the ability to think and get this done. Amen.

MORNING

## My First Priority

*"'Love the Lord your God with all your heart and with all your soul and with all your mind.' This is the first and greatest commandment."*

MATTHEW 22:37–38 NIV

Father, You are my everything! Without You, I wouldn't even be here. Forgive me for allowing so many other things to squeeze between me and You. Help me to be better about putting time with You before anything else. Talking with You gives me the strength I need to make it through the day. I love You so much! I never want to take our relationship for granted. Amen.

EVENING

## Special Words

*Thy word is a lamp unto my feet, and a light unto my path.*

PSALM 119:105 KJV

Dear heavenly Father, thank You for Your Word, the Bible. It gives me what I need to do things the right way. I'm so glad You gave us the special words in the Bible that teach us and show us how You want us to live. Help me to memorize Your words so I will have them in my heart and can rely on them all throughout my life. Amen.

DAY 350

MORNING

## God's Glory, Not Mine

*Whatever you do, do all things for the glory of God.*

1 Corinthians 10:31 NASB

Dear God, I'm really good at art. I've won prizes. My drawings are on display in the case outside the principal's office at school. People compliment me all the time about how talented I am. I always want to remember that my talent comes from You. All the prizes, compliments, and rewards belong to You. I give You the glory, Lord! When I accept those compliments, I'll be sure to give You the praise. Amen.

EVENING

## Rest

*"Come to Me, all you who labor and are heavy laden, and I will give you rest."*

Matthew 11:28 NKJV

I'm so sleepy tonight, Lord. I worked hard today. My family just moved into this new house. It took forever to unpack everything. Please take from me any worries I have about adjusting to this new place. As I close my eyes and sleep, I know You are the same God who watched over me at my old house. Everything else might have changed, but You are the same wherever I am.

MORNING

## Stop. Take a Deep Breath.

*"Seek first God's kingdom and what God wants. Then all your other needs will be met as well."*

MATTHEW 6:33 NCV

Lord, it's always rush, rush, rush. I can't seem to find time to do everything I want to do. I apologize, because sometimes I can't seem to find time just to relax and be quiet with You. I know You are with me all the time. I need to stop, take a deep breath, and let You calm my heart. When I put You first, everything else will fall into place. Amen.

EVENING

## A Blessing of Peace

*"The LORD bless you and keep you; the LORD make his face shine on you and be gracious to you; the LORD turn his face toward you and give you peace."*

NUMBERS 6:24–26 NIV

Dear heavenly Father, tonight's Bible verse is a blessing of peace. It comforts me to know that You are here right now keeping me safe. I imagine that You are looking down at me, and a warm glow of loving-kindness surrounds Your face. I'm grateful that Your thoughts always turn toward me and what I need. I feel Your love filling up my heart tonight, God. I love You too. Amen.

DAY 352

MORNING

## Never Stop Praying

*[Daniel] continued kneeling on his knees three times a day, praying and offering praise before his God, just as he had been doing previously.*

DANIEL 6:10 NASB

Father God, I've read about Daniel in my Bible. He kept right on praying when the king ruled that he couldn't. He would never stop talking with You, even if it meant he might be killed for breaking the king's rule. Daniel got down on his knees, and he prayed and prayed. Help me to be like Daniel. Whatever happens, no matter what anyone says—I will never stop praying! Amen.

EVENING

## Things Not Seen

*Now faith is the substance of things hoped for, the evidence of things not seen.*

HEBREWS 11:1 KJV

Jesus, I believe in You, but I really wish I could reach out and touch You. Believing in things I can see is easy. The Bible tells of a man named Thomas who doubted that You came back to life after You died on the cross. He saw You, and he believed. I know one day I will see You, Jesus. But in the meantime, I still believe in You. I know You are real.

MORNING

# If Only I Could Touch Him

*For [the bleeding woman] said to herself,*
*"If only I may touch His garment, I shall be made well."*
MATTHEW 9:21 NKJV

Dear Jesus, the woman in Matthew 9:21 decided she had to touch Your robe to be healed. That's how she demonstrated her faith in You. And when she touched You, You healed her. I can't physically touch You, but I can show my faith by believing and then by doing whatever You ask of me. I know You can do anything, and You are always ready to help me. Thank You! Amen.

EVENING

# Make Love Your Goal

*The goal of this command is love, which comes from a pure heart and a good conscience and a sincere faith.*
1 TIMOTHY 1:5 NIV

Dear God, I want my greatest goal to be loving others the way You love us. Love is Your greatest command. Fill me with Your perfect love, and then help me to care deeply for others. I want the love I give to come from my heart. I want to love unselfishly. Please open my eyes to the needs around me. Teach me the many ways I can show love to others. Amen.

MORNING

# Keep Your Priorities Straight

*"God is with you in all that you do."*
GENESIS 21:22 NKJV

Lord, as I go through this day, help me to keep my priorities straight. It's not all about what I do; it's also about how I treat others. Show me how to love those I come in contact with as I go through my day. Help me to be a caring person. I want Your love and who You are to shine through me, because what the world needs more of these days is You. Amen.

EVENING

# Faithful

*The Lord is faithful. He will give you strength and keep you safe from the devil.*
2 THESSALONIANS 3:3 NLV

Dear Father God, I've been thinking a lot about what it means to be faithful. You set the example by how You treat me. You show me faithfulness by never leaving me, giving up on me, or turning away from me. You always show up. You always believe in me. Thank You for teaching me about faith so I can be faithful in my relationships with others. Amen.

MORNING

# He Helps Me Grow

*He shall be like a tree planted by the rivers of water, that brings forth its fruit in its season, whose leaf also shall not wither; and whatever he does shall prosper.*

PSALM 1:23 NKJV

Dear God, I am like a tree planted near a heavenly stream. You provide my roots with water so I will grow up healthy and strong. Your Word is the "water," Lord. Reading the Bible and thinking about its words is what helps me grow in character—into the person You want me to be. Keep watering me, God! I feel my roots getting stronger each day. Amen.

EVENING

# Powerful!

*The fear of the LORD leads to life, and he who has it will abide in satisfaction; he will not be visited with evil.*

PROVERBS 19:23 NKJV

Almighty God, You are powerful beyond anything I can imagine. I'm amazed by Your power, but I'm not afraid of it. I'm not afraid, because I am Your child and You love me. Because we love each other, I don't have to be afraid of a God who rules heaven and earth. I know You will use Your power to help me, to keep me safe and make me strong. Amen.

DAY 356

MORNING

# The Main Thing

*One thing I have desired of the LORD, that will I seek: that I may dwell in the house of the LORD all the days of my life, to behold the beauty of the LORD, and to inquire in His temple.*

PSALM 27:4 NKJV

Lord, help me to remember that the main thing is to keep seeking You—to keep learning as much as I can about You and Your kingdom. Don't ever let me stop wondering about You. Remind me to ask questions about who You are and look to You for answers. Learning about You is something that will continue through my whole life. So, teach me, God. Help me to know You better.

EVENING

# A Godly Character

*And be not conformed to this world: but be ye transformed by the renewing of your mind, that ye may prove what is that good, and acceptable, and perfect, will of God.*

ROMANS 12:2 KJV

Dear God, becoming more like You doesn't just happen. You want me to work at it. When I learn what You expect from me and follow Your commands, then my personality will become more like Yours. The problem is sin. It's always lurking nearby, wanting me to follow it. If I do, then I will be less like You. Father, I want a godly character like Yours, so I will do my best to please You. Amen.

MORNING

## Busy Day

*Anxiety in the heart of man causes depression,*
*but a good word makes it glad.*
PROVERBS 12:25 NKJV

Here I am, Lord, getting ready for another busy day. Help me stay calm. I'm thinking of that famous fable about the tortoise and the hare. It taught a lesson: Slow and steady wins the race. Help me to keep an even, steady pace today. Keep me focused. Because I know that You and I will tackle this busy day together, I don't need to feel anxious. Amen.

EVENING

## Sunday

*"Remember the Day of Rest, to keep it holy.*
*Six days you will do all your work. But the seventh*
*day is a Day of Rest to the Lord your God."*
EXODUS 20:8–10 NLV

"Keep Sunday a holy day of rest." All of us are guilty of breaking that command. We go to church on Sunday and worship You; but then when we get home, we sometimes get busy with work and other stuff. You made Sunday to be a day of rest to relax and think about You and all the amazing things You've done for us. Forgive me, God, for not keeping it a holy day. Amen.

DAY 358

## MORNING

# I Will Follow You

*Then [Jesus] said to them all: "Whoever wants to be my disciple must deny themselves and take up their cross daily and follow me. For whoever wants to save their life will lose it, but whoever loses their life for me will save it."*

LUKE 9:23–24 NIV

Dear Jesus, You want me to follow You. When I read about You in the Bible—in Matthew, Mark, Luke, and John—it's like I'm following in Your footsteps. I'm listening to the words You spoke and watching how You treated others. As I read, I'm learning how to behave by following Your example. Lead me every day, Lord. Guide me all through my life. I'm ready. Amen.

## EVENING

# The Greatest Gift

*For by grace are ye saved through faith; and that not of yourselves: it is the gift of God: not of works, lest any man should boast.*

EPHESIANS 2:8–9 KJV

Dear Father God, with loving-kindness You've blessed me with many gifts, but the greatest gift of all is Jesus. You gave me Your Son. He traded His life for mine so I wouldn't be punished for not following Your commands. When You look at me now, You see Jesus in my heart. I've asked Him to live with me forever. Thank You for sharing Your Son with me. Amen.

MORNING

## Let's Grow!

*Like newborn babies, crave pure spiritual milk, so that by it you may grow up in your salvation.*

1 PETER 2:2 NIV

Heavenly Father, I'm a baby Christian right now. What I mean is that I have a whole lot more to learn about You and Jesus. The Bible will help me grow. Talking with You in prayer every day and adding to my trust and faith will also help me grow as a Christian. Step by step, day by day, teach me to follow and learn Your ways. I'm ready to learn. Let's grow! Amen.

EVENING

## The Center of God's Will

*Commit thy works unto the LORD, and thy thoughts shall be established.*

PROVERBS 16:3 KJV

Father God, I know some of what Your will for me is. I'm sure You want me to have peace, joy, and many blessings. What else? What is at the center—the most important part—of what You desire for me? I'm having trouble figuring it out. Please help me to pay attention to Your words in my heart. Show me what You want me to do and where You want me to go. Amen.

MORNING

## God with Us

*"The young woman, who has never had a man, will give birth to a Son. They will give Him the name Immanuel. This means God with us."*

MATTHEW 1:23 NLV

Dear Father, in the Bible, Jesus is also called "Immanuel," which means "God with us," and it's a reminder that Jesus is God. He is Your Son, and He lives inside our hearts. Jesus has all Your power. He can do anything! He still does miracles today just like He did when He lived on earth. He will be with me forever. Amen.

EVENING

## Rest in God

*The LORD replied, "My Presence will go with you, and I will give you rest."*

EXODUS 33:14 NIV

Jesus, troubles and challenges don't bother me much when I'm resting and at peace with You. When I come near to You in prayer, I feel the calm You give me. I am Your child, and You want to take care of me. You want me to feel safe in Your presence and rest. Now, as I lie down to sleep, help me rest in You. I'm at peace with You watching over me.

MORNING

# I Forgive–Me!

*Even so, we know we cannot become right with God by obeying the Law. A man is made right with God by putting his trust in Jesus Christ.*

GALATIANS 2:16 NLV

God, when I mess up and do what's wrong, I feel terribly guilty. I tell myself things like "You're not a good person." I want to stop doing that! When Jesus died for me, He took away my guilt. When I mess up, You have already forgiven me. I'm not right with You because I obey all the rules; I'm right with You *because of Jesus*. Help me to forgive myself more easily. Amen.

EVENING

# I Need to Forgive

*"And whenever you stand praying, if you have anything against anyone, forgive him, that your Father in heaven may also forgive you your trespasses."*

MARK 11:25 NKJV

Heavenly Father, there's someone I need to forgive. I've held on to angry feelings in my heart for a long time, and I want to let them go. I know it's the right thing to do, but it's so hard! I try, and then the feelings come back. Your Holy Spirit within me gives me the power to forgive. With Your love in my heart, I can replace my angry feelings with loving-kindness. Help me, God. Amen.

# DAY 362

## MORNING

# The Paths of Life

*"You have made known to me the paths of life;*
*you will fill me with joy in your presence."*
ACTS 2:28 NIV

Dear God, when I follow Your commands and everything turns out well, then I know I'm on the right path in life. When I make a decision, if I choose what I know is right, then I have peace in my heart and know I'm on the path You've set for me. If I follow You, God, I know You will always lead me toward what is right and good according to Your will.

## EVENING

# Loneliness

*Fear thou not; for I am with thee: be not dismayed; for I am*
*thy God: I will strengthen thee; yea, I will help thee; yea,*
*I will uphold thee with the right hand of my righteousness.*
ISAIAH 41:10 KJV

Dear Jesus, You must have felt so lonely. When You needed Your disciples to be with You in the garden the night before You were crucified, they fell asleep. When You hung dying on the cross and You didn't feel God with You, that must have been the worst kind of loneliness. When I feel lonely, Jesus, I know You understand. And I thank You for being with me. Amen.

MORNING

# The Truth

*For the message of the cross is foolishness to those who are perishing, but to us who are being saved it is the power of God.*

1 Corinthians 1:18 NIV

Jesus, there are people who refuse to believe in You. They say the Bible is like a fairy tale—it's all made up. I feel sorry for them, because they don't know the truth. You are real. When people invite You into their hearts, You change them. You give them the gift of living forever in heaven. Jesus, please help others to know the truth. I want them to believe in You and the Bible. Amen.

EVENING

# Power Boost

*He gives power to the weak, and to those who have no might He increases strength. . . . Those who wait on the Lord shall renew their strength; they shall mount up with wings like eagles, they shall run and not be weary, they shall walk and not faint.*

Isaiah 40:29, 31 NKJV

Dear God, whenever I need a power boost, I know I can count on You. If I get tired and feel like giving up, all I have to do is pray. You give me some of Your power so I can keep going. And if that power doesn't seem to come right away, I'll wait. I know it's on its way to me like a lightning bolt coming down from heaven. Amen.

DAY 364

MORNING

# I Helped a Friend Find Jesus!

*If you declare with your mouth, "Jesus is Lord," and believe in your heart that God raised him from the dead, you will be saved.*

Romans 10:9 NIV

Jesus, I helped a friend believe in You! I told her to tell her sins to You and ask for Your forgiveness. She said she believes that You are the Son of God, that You died on the cross and came to life again, and that You did it so that someday she can live with You forever in heaven. You chose her, God, and she received Your free gift of salvation. Thank You for being her Savior and Lord. Please help her to learn more about You. Amen.

EVENING

# Tears

*Put my tears into Your bottle; are they not in Your book?*

Psalm 56:8 NKJV

Dear God, in tonight's Bible verse, You were talking with King David. He said You were aware of his sadness and fear. You collected his tears in Your bottle, and You wrote about them in Your book. Then David praised You. He said he wasn't afraid. God, just as with David, You know when I cry; You count my tears; and You help my sadness and fear go away. Lord, I praise You! Amen.

## MORNING

# Strong Arms

*"The eternal God is your refuge, and underneath are the everlasting arms. He will drive out your enemies before you, saying, 'Destroy them!'"*

DEUTERONOMY 33:27 NIV

Dear heavenly Father, every day Your strong arms protect me. They hold me safely in times of trouble. I believe You will always be here for me, keeping me from harm. I trust You, God. And if I begin to doubt You, lift me up with Your strong arms and hold me tight. If people say mean things or behave badly toward me, You protect me. I love You, God. Amen.

## EVENING

# Thank You, God!

*Thanks be to God for his indescribable gift!*

2 CORINTHIANS 9:15 NIV

Thank You, God of heaven, earth, and everything in between. Thank You for using Your great power to create the earth and every living thing. Thank You for being perfectly loving, truthful, and faithful. Thank You for creating and loving me. Thank You that I can count on Your goodness because You never change. I am grateful for all You are, and I will believe and trust in You forever. Amen.

# Scripture Index

## OLD TESTAMENT

## 2 Chronicles



## Nehemiah



## Job



## Psalms

**Proverbs**

## NEW TESTAMENT